# Argonne

Barry Gregory

Editor-in-Chief: Barrie Pitt
Editor: David Mason
Art Director: Sarah Kingham
Picture Editor: Robert Hunt
Consultant Art Editor: Denis Piper
Designer: David Allen
Illustration: John Batchelor
Photographic Research: Carina Dvorak
Cartographer: Richard Natkiel

Photographs for this book were especially selected from the following archives: from left to right pages 2-3 US National Archives, Washington; 7 Etablisement Cinematographique et Photographique des Armees, France; 8-9 National Archives; 10 Bundesarchiv, Koblenz; 10 Bayer Hauptstaatsarchiv, Munchen; 11 Imperial War Museum, London; 12 Roger Viollet, Paris; 12 Radio Times-Hulton Picture Library, London; 12 Viollet; 14 National Archives; 14-15 Bundesarchiv; 14-15 National Archives of Canada, Ottawa; 15 ECPA; 16 Viollet; 17 IWM; 18-21 National Archives; 22 IWM; 24 National Archives; 26 Viollet; 28-29 Musee de la Guerre, France; 30 ECPA; 31 Viollet; 31-32 National Archives; 34-36 National Archives; 36-37 IWM; 37.Ullstein GmbH, Berlin; 38 IWM; 40-41 Viollet; 40 Suddeutscher Verlag, Munchen; 41 Viollet; 42 National Archives; 50-51 Viollet; 52-53 National Archives; 53-56 Viollet; 56-57 National Archives; 58 IWM; 60-61 Viollet; 60 National Archives; 61 Ullstein; 62-63 ECPA; 64 National Archives; 66-67 IWM; 67-68 National Archives; 70-71 IWM; 73 ECPA; 73-81 National Archives; 82-83 Ullstein; 84 National Archives; 84-85 Suddeutscher Verlag; 87 IWM; 88-89 Viollet; 92-93 National Archives; 94IWM; 95-106 National Archives; 108 IWM; 108-118 National Archives; 122 IWM; 122-123 Viollet; 123 IWM; 124-125 National Archives; 125 Wehrgeschichtliches Museum, Rastadt; 126-131 National Archives; 132-133 IWM; 134-135 National Archives; 136-150 National Archives; 150-151 National Archives of Canada; 152 Viollet; 153 Bundesarchiv; 154 National Archives; 154-155 Ullstein; 155 Viollet; 156 Bundesarchiv; 157 National Archives; 158-159 Documentation Francaise, France. Front and back cover: US National Archives, Washington.

**Copyright** © Ballantine Books Inc. 1972

First Printing: **December** 1972
Printed in United States of America

Ballantine Books Inc.
101 Fifth Avenue New York NY10003

An Intext Publisher

# Contents

6 Introduction
8 'Tout le monde à la bataille'
20 The Foch Plan
28 'When are the Yanks coming?'
38 Training in Lorraine
50 Into line
66 The Aisne-Marne counter-offensive
74 The way to the Argonne
92 The Argonne-Meuse offensive
148 Springboard to victory
160 Bibliography

# 'The Yanks are coming...'

When Europe went to war in 1914, it did so in a mood of joyous certainty. Both sides were confident that their causes were just, that their armies were invincible, and that their consequent victories would be glorious, overwhelming and practically immediate. So inexhaustible are the springs of human optimism that it was some time before the nations as a whole realised that the war was not progressing in accordance with their first ingenuous suppositions, and that they would be called upon to pay for their days of splendid ardour throughout the years of pain and anguish. National reserves of fortitude and endurance were to be drawn upon to the full, and Germany's dominance among the Central Powers increased as time passed.

Among the Allies, however, the relative seniorities of the partners subtly altered. Russia and France had possessed the enormous forces which first flung themselves upon the enemy in August 1914, when Britain's contribution was her Navy (in Continental eyes of no account) and an original expeditionary force so small that her own propagandists coined the historic appellation 'contemptible little army', and then attributed its origin to her foes. Time was to alter this, and by 1916 Britain had an army in the field which Germany recognised as the major block to Kaiserlich ambitions. Britain had thus replaced France as the senior partner on the Western Front; but although the power had changed hands, the philosophy remained the same.

For years before the war, the official policy of the French army had been based upon the 'Spirit of the Offensive' with which their soldiers had been thoroughly imbued – and time and occasion combined to infect their British ally with the same principles. When, eventually, the French were to pause and reflect upon the wisdom of their creed, their erstwhile junior partners regarded them with a disdain not unmixed with malice, and assumed the tradition of the offensive themselves. Victory, however, still eluded them, but in a moment of doubtful inspiration was produced the 'Doctrine of Attrition' which, if lacking in imagination, possessed the supreme appeal of simplicity. All it required for its operation and success was an unlimited supply of men for the trenches – and Britain's Empire was vast.

But by the end of 1917, it was becoming evident that even Britain could not afford such wild extravagance as that in which her army commanders had been indulging. True, the enemy had suffered considerably as a result of the vast conflicts which had been forced upon her, but despite these losses there was as yet little sign of disintegration among the Central Powers. Russia's losses had been even greater than Germany's. France's losses had come near to crippling her. Europe was thus on the verge of bankruptcy: a bankruptcy far more vitiating than one to be declared in some centre of commercial law, for it was of blood and spirit, of manhood and human hopes.

Grim despondency was the mood which now dominated the peoples of the warring nations. Not yet plunged into defeatism, they were unable to perceive the means of victory.

Yet two events had occurred in 1917 which seemed to offer the golden prize, first to the Central Powers, then to the Allies.

In March had begun the Russian Revolution. It did not immediately release German and Austrian divisions from the Eastern Front, and indeed the Russian General Brusilov was to launch yet another offensive against them. But it was obvious to the German rulers that by early 1918 they should be able to concentrate their strength in the West. In order to expedite the Russian collapse, the German government even allowed the passage of Lenin across the country ('in a sealed carriage, like some dangerous bacillus'), for they knew that if they were to grasp their chance of victory, they must do it quickly. Germany's chance was *now*, for in April had occurred the second event which might well serve to snatch victory from her: America had entered the war, and her vast potential of men and materials would undoubtedly tip the scales against the Central Powers if given the time to do so. So it became a race, *against* time for Germany, *for* time for Britain and France.

As 1918 dawned, half in fear and half in hope, Europe looked towards America. She alone seemed to possess the key to the situation. Whether she would arrive in time to turn the scales was another matter.

# 'Tout le monde à la bataille'

In the Spring of 1918 the strength of the German army in the West was estimated at 217 divisions; not counting forty-eight Austro-Hungarian divisions employed for the most part on the Italian Front. The Treaty of Brest-Litovsk had led to the release of forty-four victorious German divisions from the Russian Front for service in France. The German divisions then in the West approximated a total of 3,000,000 men.

The manpower potential still remaining in Germany was sufficient to raise another thirty divisions. The morale of the German soldiers was high. Almost the whole combat strength of the German army was deployed in the Spring offensive. As von Hutier's shock divisions, veterans of the Riga campaign of 1917, broke out from St Quentin, victory must surely have seemed within Ludendorff's grasp.

With twelve Belgian, four American and two Portuguese divisions in the field, the Allies could muster at this time 188 divisions or about 2,600,000 men, with a ratio of three French to every two British divisions. The Italians needed all the troops they could find on their own front; and, with the advent of Soviet power astutely assisted by Wilhelmine political stratagem, no help could be

expected from Russia. Although one observer put the German advantage in combat capability at only ten per cent, Allied morale was at a low ebb. The British and French soldiers in 1918 were on the whole too old, too young or inadequately trained for battle. No wonder Pétain believed the war was lost.

In the ensuing months after his prompt decision at Doullens to bolster the British front with French divisions and fight before Amiens, Foch enforced his policy of 'defiance no matter the cost' with superb *élan*. As each new offensive threatened defeat for the Allies, Foch held one trump card and laid it face-up on the table for all to see. The face on the card was that of General John J Pershing, United States Army. Since January the Germans had watched the build-up of American forces with concern. Their Spring offensive had been designed to beat the British before the American Expeditionary Force developed into a fighting army.

On 28th March General Pershing, alarmed at the collapse of the British Fifth Army, offered to throw his four trained divisions into battle. (These troops had been held in reserve pending the formation of I Corps AEF as a national unit of 380,000 men.) With no evidence of the emotional reserve that had earned taciturn 'Black Jack' Pershing his nickname, he addressed Pétain and his generals at French Headquarters at Clermont-sur-Oise in their own language, giving them *carte blanche* to make use of American resources:

'... *infanterie, artillerie, aviation, tout ce que nous avons est à vous. Disposez-en comme il vous plaira* ...'

General Pétain accepted the American general's offer with alacrity. In the event, few artillery pieces of American design were made in the factories in the United States and American gunners and tank crews were trained to handle French, British and some American-adapted equipment. Furthermore, in March Pershing had little ordnance and no American planes had arrived on French airfields.

From 6th April 1917, the date the United States entered the European conflict to the date of Pershing's meeting with Pétain only 300,000 American troops – including rear personnel – had disembarked on French soil. But by the end of July, when victory favoured the Allies on the Marne, the number of American

**Survivors of Major Whittlesey's 'Lost Battalion' of the US 308th Infantry Regiment rest near Apremont in the Argonne Forest, October 1918**

*Above:* Victorious German troops prepare to advance on the Compiègne Forest during Operation Gneisenau. *Below:* Von Hutier's shock troops proved themselves against the Russians at Riga in the summer of 1917 and later formed the spearhead of the German spring offensive on the Western Front. *Right:* British and French troops lie waiting in a hastily-prepared defensive position during the German spring offensive

*Above left:* General Erich von Ludendorff. His troops launched five major offensives in the spring and summer of 1918 before they were halted by the French and Americans on the Marne in July. *Below left:* Marshal Ferdinand Foch. *Above:* 'Black Jack' Pershing. *Below:* General Philippe Pétain. Under Foch he remained in tactical control of the French army at the battle front

soldiers in France had risen astronomically to 1,500,000 men. Since March the Germans had suffered 800,000 casualties, and were completely demoralised. The last reserve divisions had already been committed to the front line. Numbers on the opposing sides were about equal, but another 500,000 men were already under arms in the United States. The time was approaching for Foch to play his trump card: Pershing's Expeditionary Force and the seemingly unlimited resources in manpower of the American Draft Board.

Jubilant at the impending collapse of the Aisne-Marne salient, Foch met with his principal commanders on 24th July at Pershing's Headquarters at Chaumont in an optimistic mood. Supported by such vast reserve potential and material advantage in planes, tanks and artillery, the time had arrived to lead the way to the great onslaught on the line from Flanders to Verdun. The immediate scheme that emerged provided for both tactical and economic benefits. Direct rail communication between Paris and Amiens was prevented by the salient. Similarly the rail-link between Paris and the Lorraine border was impeded by the Aisne – Marne bulge and by the guns in the St Mihiel salient in the area of Commercy. Two offensives were planned at once to seize these stretches of railway and wipe out the offending salients. Further attacks were foreseen having in view the recapture of coalfields in the north by driving the enemy from the areas of Dunkirk and Calais.

The Anglo-French offensive called for in early August sought therefore to iron out the start-line for a hammer blow on the Hindenburg Line; and in so doing take revenge for the March defeat on the Arras – St Quentin sector. Freeing the Paris – Verdun track was made the minimum requirement of the Franco-American operations in progress on the Marne. An American offensive was scheduled for a month later to release the Verdun – Avricourt track and reach the Haudiomont – Pont-à-Mousson base line of the St Mihiel salient. This latter attack, which Pershing gladly took on, was limited in purpose to permit later action on a larger scale between the Meuse and the Moselle. The Heights of the Meuse in the south of the bulge overlooked the Briey ironfields and the Metz fortress across the plain of the Woëvre. Although weakened in defence by the distribution of its artillery to the front line, Metz was an important depot for the assembly of supplies from Germany. Through Metz flowed the life-blood of the German supply system south of the Ardennes by rail to Lille and Bruges.

On 8th August Rawlinson's British Fourth Army, using the Byng 'Cambrai tactics' of 1917, attacked eastwards from the Ancre on a ten-mile front. Without ranging shots 2,000 guns broke the silence and under cover of a rolling barrage 600 tanks lumbered into action. Seventeen infantry and three cavalry divisions, including the Canadian and Australian Corps and two American divisions, followed closely behind. Overhead 800 aircraft flew on reconnaissance and bombing missions. Crossing the Somme the same day, popularly known as Ludendorff's 'Black Day', entire German units went to pieces in the face of the oncoming tanks. In two days the British cavalry and the two Dominion Corps were twelve miles on, and the approach march to the Hindenburg Line had begun.

The following day Debeney's French First Army on Rawlinson's right moved off south of the Luce and took Montdidier. Debeney had ten divisions, few tanks, but 1,100 planes in the air. Next Humbert's French Third Army exerted pressure on the southern curve of the bulge at Noyon. Still further south Mangin's French Tenth Army west of Soissons gave valuable support by taking the Heights of the Aisne. Although Debeney's progress was at first less spectacular, he was not far behind Raw-

*Above:* General Byng, commander of the British Third Army
*Below:* Demoralised prisoners from Gough's luckless Fifth Army are marched through St Quentin

*Above:* British 60-pounders in action during the Battle of Amiens, August 1918. *Below:* General Mangin, commander of the French Tenth Army

**General Humbert, commander of the French Third Army**

linson, and Humbert rapidly drove northwards. Disagreement over the choice of an intermediate Anglo-French objective now induced Foch to remove Debeney's army from Haig's overall direction.

On 21st August Haig sent forward Byng's Third Army on Rawlinson's left with tank support north of Albert, and held back reserves to meet a German counterattack that came two days later on the centre of the British Front. Haig's anticipation of the event resulted in a general advance on a thirty-mile front. Von der Marwitz's Second and von Hutier's Eighteenth Armies fell back in disorder. Byng, swinging outwards for Bapaume, was joined on his left by Horne's British First Army extending the line northwards. As Rawlinson in the centre steam-rollered on to Péronne, the Anglo-French front expanded seventy miles from Arras to the Aisne.

At the end of the month the Australians triumphantly stormed Mont St Quentin and the Canadians on the Scarpe broke through east of Arras. Although the Canadians had overrun a link known as the Drocourt-Quéant Switch, the Allies halted on 3rd September at a system of constructed defences that stretched from Lille to Metz. The bastion of the network of ferro-concrete fortifications, which now confronted the British army beyond a line Bapaume – St Quentin, was named the *Siegfried-Stellung* or Hindenburg Line.

Another outcome of the Chaumont conference on 24th July was the announcement of the organisation of the American First Army. This army was actually established on 10th August, and Pershing and his staff set about the task of planning the St Mihiel battle from his headquarters

**Australians share a trench with dead Germans in the St Quentin area, late August**

twenty miles west of the salient. Disregarding Foch's suggestion for reinforcing the power of the offensive with a second Franco-American army under French command, he declined also the services on his staff of General Degoutte as tactical consultant. While the AEF went into training for its first operation as a national army, 3,000 guns, 267 light tanks and 1,500 aircraft were assembled with the help of British, French, Italian and Portuguese units. The French II Colonial Corps was assigned to act in concert with I, IV and V Corps AEF. Meanwhile 'Army Group Gallwitz' ordered a September withdrawal from the salient to the Michel Position; which ran parallel to the base line and formed the eastern end of the German fortified defence system on the Western Front. Von Gallwitz had expected an American attack at St Mihiel since the Marne counteroffensive of 18th July.

When on 12th September Pershing's artillery bombardment opened up, von Fuch's Army Unit C – a mixed bag of front line, reserve and *Landwehr* troops – was busy removing machine-gun posts and transporting stores to the rear. Nine divisions including an Austro-Hungarian (*Kaiserlich und Königliche*) division gave only brief opposition. Although like Shiloh and Antietam the battle was virtually over in a day, the swift but sure Franco-American victory was nonetheless commendable. As French divisions surrounding the head of the triangle edged forward, French and American troops swept across the area from both sides. The 26th (Yankee) Division, flanked on either side by the French, fought its way from the western start-line to meet seven American divisions advancing from the south and east. The final rendezvous was made on high ground at the village of Vigneulles overlooking the base line of the triangle. All objectives were taken by the evening of the 13th, and the last shots fired three days later.

*Above:* A German trench mortar position taken by Summerall's 1st Division on the second day of the Soissons offensive in July. *Right:* The German Crown Prince (seated right) visits the headquarters of General von Conta on the first day of the spring offensive

As the eager Americans scanned the plain of the Woëvre from vantage points on the Meuse heights, in their mind's eye they saw Berlin and not the Metz conurbation before them. The idea held by some that the winter training programme would see off the less able officers and mean promotion for the rest for the Spring onslaught on the Rhine was not shared by the most senior commanders. The American First Army had ten days in which to form up with its full resources on a twenty-mile front running from the western edge of the Argonne Forest to the Meuse river. The Foch Plan for victory brooked no delay. Before the month was out the autumnal light was speckled with leaves swirling helplessly in rhythm with the rattle of machine-gun fire and fall of high explosive shot of the Argonne-Meuse offensive.

# The Foch Plan

In 1914 Germany had swiftly achieved at least one of her war aims: control of the heavily industrialised region of northern France. As the war progressed and the Allied naval blockade increased its stranglehold on the Central Powers, the exploitation of captured French resources was all the more vital. Deprived of trade-links with most neutral countries and her vanished colonial empire, Germany's enormous hold on French steel, iron, coal, wool and sugar production was important bounty. But after the failure of the five offensives the German war machine needed more than raw materials to sustain its effort; a defence plan was imperative to prevent the Allies marching on the Fatherland.

There were five areas that the Germans were most reluctant to evacuate:

1 The Flanders littoral, where their bases for submarines and bombing planes were situated. The German U-Boat was an effective offensive as well as defensive weapon in the economic battle of wits being waged on the high seas.

2 The defended area of Lille was essential to the security of the Flanders coast. Lille had hitherto been the marshalling yard of reinforcements and supplies for the great battles on the British front from Ypres to St

**Part of Patton's 1st Tank Brigade, equipped with light French Renaults**

Quentin. The depot city now fed the Hindenburg Line.

3 The Metz – Mézières – Hirson – Valenciennes – Lille railway, which was the great lateral supply route south of the Ardennes. (This line, which branches at Maubeuge for Brussels, Ghent and Bruges, thus also penetrates almost to the Flanders coast.)

4 The north-south defended area Thionville – Metz was a stronghold protecting the German frontier in Lorraine. The rail centre of Metz is connected directly with Strasbourg in Alsace and the interior of Germany.

5 The front line from Metz to Switzerland, which almost coincided with the German frontier. Although stalemate existed on this front, a close watch was always kept on both sides. For geographical reasons any Allied offensive eastwards of the Moselle though was hardly likely.

The periphery of occupied France was edged by a series of zonal defence positions extending from Lille to Metz. In September 1917 Hindenburg and Ludendorff ordered that this new system of defences should be constructed from Arras through St Quentin to the neighbourhood of Vailly on the Aisne. But although the Siegfried Position (Hindenburg Line) was over fifty miles long it was also part of a much wider defence system. Northwards along the Canal du Nord the Wotan Position (Drocourt – Quéant Switch) went on thirty miles to Lille. Eastwards along the line of the Aisne to Verdun ran the Alberich and Brunhilde Positions. Brunhilde was flanked by Kriemhilde, which had the Argonne Forest as its formidable bastion. Further east still the Michel Position embraced the Metz fortress at the head of a spur that curled northwards to Thionville on the Moselle. Hundung was built in the rear of Alberich as a western arm of the Brunhilde Position. Behind this

**German prisoners**

again from the Flanders frontier near Valenciennes to the Meuse south-east of Sedan were the Hermann – Hagen – Freya Positions. Alberich – Hundung – Hagen lay back forty miles at the deepest point. The fortified area in the north was additionally protected by a maze of river lines and canals.

The Siegfried defences, built by the hard labour of Russian prisoners, conscripted civilians and the German soldiers themselves, were a masterpiece of mass-produced fortification. Specialist advice was recruited from the German factories to make the ferro-concrete dug-outs and emplacements, and woodwork was turned out to pattern in the sawmills. Although the core of the Hindenburg Line was some 8,000 yards in depth, its overall depth was at least double that measurement. Like a grey Hadean chessboard with a mass of superimposed obstacles of diverse pattern, the total area of the position was sectioned off into zones. In the battle zone in the centre, the squares of the board contained concrete machine-gun emplacements. In the advanced area the out-post zone some 600 yards deep denied the attacker observation over it. In front of the out-post zone lay a strong entrenchment or line of piquets, with light machine-guns housed in shallow concrete dug-outs. Three lines of barbed-wire were usually placed zig-zag fashion in front of the fire trench, and machine-guns sited at the points of the re-entrant angles so that the gunners could sweep from side to side. In the reserve areas behind the battle zone there were artillery protection and support zones. Maximum use was made of reverse slopes for siting guns: observation posts were protected; tunnels were made and a light railway system served the position.

Although Foch continued to urge the British and American commanders to strengthen their forces for the decisive effort in 1919, he had nursed the idea of a general offensive in September 1918 since before the victory on the Marne. Encouraged still further by the August victory in the Battle of Amiens, the principles of a general offensive agreed by Foch, Pétain, Haig and Pershing at Chaumont emerged more clearly as actual September assignments. In simple terms these were defined from north to south as offensive in Flanders; western pincer (Cambrai – St Quentin); pressure on the French centre and southern pincer (Argonne – Meuse). By far the most important feature of this strategic plan was the giant pincer movement designed to break through the Armentières – Verdun curve to envelop the German army. Undeterred by the formidable German defensive system, the Allies chose to pierce it by bold assault at two of its strongest points. The Siegfried Position grimly confronted the northern sector; and in the south the Argonne had been cherished for centuries by the French themselves as a symbol of impregnability. Moreover the Germans enhanced its apparent reputation in 1915 by turning the wooded ridge into a heavily fortified position. But the advantage in combat strength, *matériel* and morale was now plainly with the Allies.

Ludendorff's 197 divisions were all below strength; only one in four being classified by the Allies as 'effective fighting formations'. Civil uproar and near starvation on the home front had undermined what spirit was left in the front line troops. On Ludendorff's 'Black Day' (8th August) German troops retreating on the Somme abused the relief columns as servants of the professional military fanatics. Foch had at his disposal 102 French, 60 British, 42 American, 12 Belgian, 2 Italian and 2 Portuguese divisions. The American divisions were at full strength; and, it will be remembered, about twice the size of the other Allied divisions. Morale had never been higher in the Allied armies. Although civilian belts in Britain and France were tightly fastened, with American resources also behind them, the balance of economic power was tipped steeply in favour of the Allies. Everything pointed to a swift pincer movement that would trap the German army before it could escape from France. Once the wall was breached in the north and south, the Germans could exercise little flexibility in defence. In spite of some well-equipped counterattack divisions, the German reserves were inadequate to meet a strong converging movement from the entire length of the line.

Ludendorff might well evade the pincer grip by rapid withdrawal along well-mapped escape routes to the German frontier; but he would not easily reconcile the loss of valuable stores and equipment. The ruthless demolition of roads and railways would nevertheless compel the Allies to build new supply lines to support their advance. The essence of the Foch Plan was to prevent the orderly, step-by-step retreat of the German army, as well as the erasure of useful lines of communication. The Germans relied for logistic support (and would have to defend for evacuation) on three rail routes to the rear of their lines. In addition to the lateral east-west supply route Strasbourg – Metz – Mézières – Maubeuge – Lille – Bruges, a northerly route running from Cologne via Liège and Namur ended at Maubeuge, fifteen miles south of the Belgian frontier. In the east Koblenz was connected to the 'back door' at Virton in the southern part of the Luxembourg province of Belgium. A British-French offensive (western pincer) was to drive eastwards to Aulnoye, a few miles south of Maubeuge on the Metz line. The junction town of Aulnoye, of easy access to Cambrai and Arras, directly supplied the battle front at St Quentin. Another offensive (southern pincer), French-American, was ultimately aimed at Mézières in the Ardennes, a second vital distribution point for front line supplies some sixty miles east of Aulnoye.

Foch planned aggressive action by all his front line divisions in support of the pincer movement. The timing of each attack was staggered in the hope of throwing the deployment of enemy reserves into confusion.

On 26th September a French-American attack was to be launched northwards as the southern arm of the pincer on the general line Reims – Verdun, advancing between the Suippe and Meuse rivers. The French Fourth Army (Gouraud) in the west manned hilly, rock-strewn terrain from the Suippe to the western edge of the Argonne Forest. Pershing's American First Army sector extended from the forest area to the Meuse heights on the east bank of the river. The village of Grandpré, north of the Argonne Forest in the Bourgogne Wood, was made the assembly point for a combined advance by the two armies on the Mézières – Sedan – Serignac portion of the important rail route to the north. The offensive was to be mounted by thirty-seven divisions, 500 light tanks and air superiority was assured. The Germans had twenty-four divisions in the front line and twelve in reserve.

In mid-September Byng's Third and Rawlinson's Fourth Armies, advancing between Bapaume and Péronne, were ordered to clear outlying defence lines of the Siegfried Position; which resulted in battles at Havrincourt and Epéhy. On 27th September the Third operating with Horne's First Army on the left, were to cross the Canal du Nord and sweep down over the St Quentin canal to the Siegfried Position from the north. Twenty-seven divisions were involved. The greater share of the British allotment of 1,500 heavy guns, 1,100 planes and fourteen tank battalions went to the Fourth Army, which was to join the offensive two days later.

On 28th September King Albert's Army, comprising twelve Belgian, six French and ten British divisions, was to move forward to Ghent between Armentières and the sea. The French and British divisions were of the French Sixth and the British Second Armies. Plumer's Second Army was stationed on the right in its bleak, shell-torn *logement* in Flanders in the Ypres salient. Birdwood's reconstituted British Fifth Army was held in reserve covering the gap between the army groups commanded by King Albert and Field Marshal Haig. There were twenty-four German divisions on King Albert's front.

On 29th September Rawlinson's Fourth and Debeney's First Armies would make a frontal assault on the Siegfried Position. Twenty-nine British, French and two American divisions were distributed along the front between Epéhy (near Péronne) and La Fère; the French on the right as far as La Fère on the Oise. Three British and one French army were therefore to act in co-ordinated movement as the western arm of the pincer. Opposing German forces were about equal; about one third of their total divisions being held in reserve.

On the more passive central front – between Debeney on the left and Gouraud on the right – were two more French armies. Berthelot's Fifth and Mangin's Tenth Armies of twenty-eight divisions would carry out probing attacks and make limited advances to activate the whole length of the line from the North Sea to the Meuse. Although Foch had an idea for a later strike on either side of Metz, de Castelnau's French Army Group east of the Meuse played only a defensive role during the closing weeks of the war. Bullard's American Second Army, covering Liggett's right between the Meuse and the Moselle, did however make some progress along the Woëvre plain.

Our spotlight now turns on the American Expeditionary Force and the southern offensive of 26th September when the other *tour de force* was seen in the Argonne. Here about half a million American soldiers, most al-

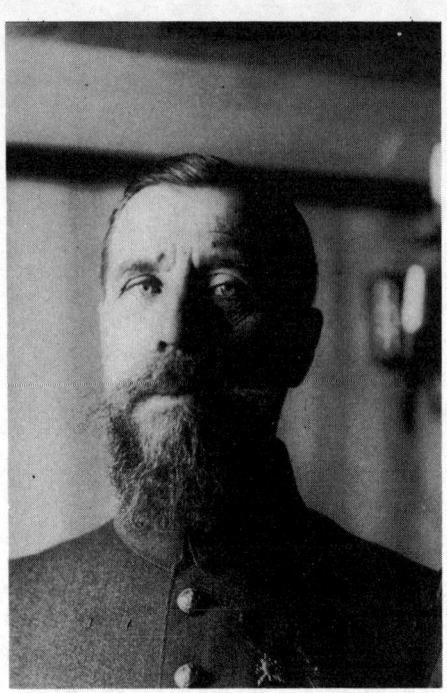

*Above:* General Gouraud, commander of the French Fourth Army. *Below:* Field-Marshal Sir Douglas Haig, British C-in-C

*Above:* General Hunter Liggett, commander of US First Army. *Below:* General Robert L Bullard, commander of US Second Army

most as new to soldiers' uniforms as they were to the European environment, jostled on the twenty-mile Encouraged still further by the August victory in the Battle of Amiens, the principles of a general offensive agreed by Foch, Pétain, Haig and Pershing at Chaumont emerged more clearly as actual September assignments. In simple terms these were defined from north to south as offensive in Flanders; western pincer (Cambrai – St Quentin); pressure on the French centre and southern pincer (Argonne – Meuse). By far the most important feature of this strategic plan was the giant pincer movement designed to break through the Armentières – Verdun curve to envelop the German army. Undeterred by the formidable German defensive system, the Allies chose to pierce it by bold assault at two of its strongest points. The Siegfried Position grimly confronted the northern sector; and in the south the Argonne had been cherished for centuries by the French themselves as a symbol of impregnability. Moreover the Germans enhanced its apparent reputation in 1915 by turning the wooded ridge into a heavily fortified position. But the advantage in combat strength, *matériel* and morale was now plainly with the Allies.

Ludendorff's 197 divisions were all below strength; only one in four being classified by the Allies as 'effective fighting formations'. Civil uproar and near starvation on the home front had undermined what spirit was left in the front line troops. On Ludendorff's 'Black Day' (8th August) German troops retreating on the Somme abused the relief columns as servants of the professional military fanatics. Foch had at his disposal 102 French, 60 British, 42 American, 12 Belgian, 2 Italian and 2 Portuguese divisions. The American divisions were at full strength; and, it will be remembered, about twice the size of the other Allied divisions. Morale had never been higher in the Allied armies. Although civilian belts in Britain and France were tightly fastened, with American resources also behind them, the balance of economic power was tipped steeply in favour of the Allies. Everything pointed to a swift pincer movement that would trap the German army before it could escape from France. Once the wall was breached in the north and south, the Germans could exercise little flexibility in defence. In spite of some well-equipped counterattack divisions, the German reserves were inadequate to meet a strong converging movement from the entire length of the line.

Ludendorff might well evade the pincer grip by rapid withdrawal along well-mapped escape routes to the German frontier; but he would not easily reconcile the loss of valuable stores and equipment. The ruthless demolition of roads and railways front Argonne Forest – Meuse River. The start-line roughly bisected the 1,150ft forest ridge, which is ten miles wide, and dipped steeply into the Meuse valley. The deeply-ravined forest locale bristled with well-concealed German artillery and machine-gun battalions. In the valley alongside the ridge the attackers before Montfaucon Wood lay in a kind of *cul-de-sac* formed by the ridge on the left and the river and the Meuse heights on the right. Behind the German front a distance of eight miles from Montfaucon rose the Romagne and Cunel heights and the man-made Kriemhilde position. What Verdun had been to the French, the Argonne now was to the Germans. The functions of the two bastions of their respective defensive systems bore a striking resemblance in reverse. But the French cry at Verdun of 'They shall not pass' echoed now by German voices in the Argonne, was not heard by Pershing's soldiers marching jauntily through the night to the front line. Unlike their more wary combat-tested allies in the north, the American infantry wheeled into line and advanced overtly with the innocent defiance of bygone days of Austerlitz and Borodinó.

# 'When are the Yanks coming?'

General Pershing's determination that the AEF would not merely provide piecemeal reinforcements for French and British divisions was greeted with impatient gestures by the members of the Supreme War Council. The General wished to create and preserve the national identity of the men under his command as an independent army in front line operations. After all the British had insisted on the same privilege in 1914; but Pershing bought time to assemble his army at the expense of his popularity at the conference table. After his arrival in Paris in June 1917 he had to select a region suitable for the training and deployment of an army numbered perhaps in millions of men, establish a sound command structure, obtain modern weapons and equipment, construct depots, develop lines of supply and build base hospitals. Pershing reached an agreement with the French authorities by 1st July on the coordination of the war effort. His message to Newton Diehl Baker at the War Department in Washington was simple. 'I need at least three million men to complete the job in two years.'

Back at home General Hugh L Scott, the army's Chief-of-Staff, had already persuaded President Wilson, War Secretary Baker and Congress to adopt a universal Military Draft Law. The Selective Service Act of 18th May 1917 required all men between the ages of twenty-one and thirty inclusive to register for service, the age limits being extended in 1918 to between eighteen and forty-five. Newton D Baker, ex-Mayor of Cleveland and a man of deep pacifist convictions, embarked on the vigorous administration of a $15 billion military programme. 10,000,000 men were enrolled, and of the 4,000,000 recruits inducted into the army, just over half set sail for Europe before the armistice in November 1918. Fears of a repetition of the draft riots of 1863 proved unfounded: over fifty per cent of the divisions raised were all-volunteer National Guard and Regular Army, as opposed to the conscript National Army. On the home front financier Bernard M Baruch was made chairman of the National Defense Commission on Raw Materials, Minerals, and Metals, and in time mobilised American industry as Chairman of the War Industries Board. Herbert C Hoover returned from organizing relief for starving civilians in German-occupied Belgium and northern France to act as the national food administrator and stock the American larder. Although at first public interest in the war was slight, publicist George Creel of the Committee on Public Information moulded public opinion in a well-directed propaganda campaign. 70,000 'four-minute' men fired off a barrage of patriotic oratory in public places and indignation was aroused by alleged German atrocities. The revolutionary spirits of Molly Pitcher and Margaret Corbin mingled with the patriot women marchers in busy urban thoroughfares.

In April Pershing's original army stood at 200,000 men. 133,000 'regulars' were in service in cantonments and posts located mainly in eastern and southern states as far apart as New York State and the Mexican border. 77,000 citizen-élite national guardsmen were hard at work in their farms, at factory benches and in offices throughout the nation. As slightly bewildered civilians were handed their numbered registration cards at the offices of nearly 5,000 local draft

boards, groups of regular soldiers and marines seen at railroad stations en route for eastern ports were rewarded with improved professional status as 'regulars'.

The state-organized National Guard, evolved from the militia of colonial days, was swiftly brought under federal control. The National Guard, a title assumed in 1824 on escort duty for America's favoured guest, the Marquis de Lafayette, had been mobilized in the War of 1812 and again in 1898 in the Spanish-American war. Many national guardsmen had seen action with Pershing against the Villistas and regular Mexican troops in the border operations of 1916-17. Of the forty-two full divisions eventually raised in the United States, eight were Regular Army, seventeen National Guard and seventeen National Army.

In early June the nucleus of the infantry of the regular 1st Expeditionary Division (Major-General William L Sibert) arrived in New York City from posts on the Mexican border,

*Left:* **Doughboys meet with French soldiers at a training camp in Lorraine.**
*Right:* **Training in digging trenches.**
*Below:* **Call up**

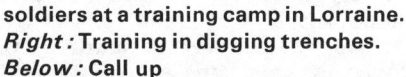

**Many of the early arrivals in France had seen action with Pershing in the Mexican punitive expedition of 1916–1917**

Washington Barracks and Fort Oglethorpe. Engineer Sibert, who came from the Panama Canal Zone, commanded the division until December 1917 when Major-General Robert L Bullard assumed command. Divisional Headquarters and the first contingent sailed on 14th June from New York and Hoboken for St Nazaire. On that day also the 5th Marines of the regular 2nd Division embarked at Philadelphia for the same destination. These first troops to arrive in France celebrated 4th July with a parade along the Champs Elysées in Paris. The second contingent of three regiments of field artillery and the signal battalion of the 1st Expeditionary Division followed six weeks later. Although the movement of the division overseas was not completed until December, the systematic training of the 1st and 2nd Infantry and 1st Field Artillery Brigades started in France on the last day of August. The remainder of the 4th Marine Brigade (Infantry) formed at Quantico, the 3rd Infantry Brigade and engineer and artillery units of the 2nd Division drawn from widespread sources sailed in late September. A detachment of the 5th Marines was already in training in France by this time. Major-General Omar Bundy took over command of the division on 8th November.

The 26th (Yankee) Division (Major-General Clarence R Edwards) was formed from the National Guard of New England. The men were said to be of more than average height, broad-chested and vigorous. Pride of locality endured in regiments with Civil War and Revolutionary traditions. Friends and neighbours soldiered together.

The division was at first concentrated in transit camps in Massachusetts, Connecticut, Rhode Island and Charlotte, North Carolina. When the volunteer division started to move overseas on 6th September extra ports of embarkation were brought into use at Newport News and Montreal. Elements of the 51st Infantry Brigade including many men from Boston and a field artillery regiment were soon ashore at Liverpool and St Nazaire and commenced training in France only a few weeks after the regulars of the renamed 1st Division. Troops failing to salute their divisional commander received personal instruction from the general. 'You don't salute your superior officer? Well your general salutes you in order to show you how to salute!'

The last of the four pioneer divisions to embark for the war, and which were to form the bulk of I Corps AEF in the early days was the celebrated 42nd (Rainbow) Division. This National Guard division was thus-named for the 'All-American' breadth of selection of its units. Major-General William A Mann was succeeded in the command of the division in December by artilleryman Major-General Charles T Menoher. Colonel Douglas MacArthur, of greater fame in the Second World War, served as Chief-of-Staff and led the 84th Infantry Brigade for the last three months of the war. Units drawn from twenty-six states were concentrated on 20th August at Camp Mills, New York, where the 83rd and 84th Infantry, and the 67th Field Artillery Brigades with Divisional Troops were formed. With 27,000 officers and men assembled on 8th October, Mann's division was almost at full strength before leaving the United States. The majority of these National Guardsmen moved into their training area in France in early November. The hard core of America's professionals and peacetime volunteers were therefore training in earnest in European conditions in the winter of 1917. The only American disappointed with progress so far was the self-styled 'Colonel' Theodore Roosevelt. With memories of his Rough Riders and the charge at Kettle Hill on the road to Santiago, the ex-President's Churchillian offer to raise a division of horse riflemen recruited from friends and admirers was declined by 'that villain Wilson'.

As the crowded troop transport

**Major-General Omar Bundy, commander of US 2nd Division**

ships nosed out of New York Bay and other North American sally-ports to brave the Atlantic supply lanes to Britain and France, they were joined by naval escort vessels on anxious watch for German submarines. Hoboken, New Jersey, opposite Manhattan on the Hudson River almost became the byword for seemingly-frustrated hopes of the Kaiser's defeat on the Western Front.

In April 1917 the United States navy owned only three transports; merchantmen and freighters had to be chartered to get the first troop contingent across to St Nazaire in June. Almost half the transport tonnage used in the next eighteen months was British; and starting with the *Vaterland* (*Leviathan*) over half a million troops were carried in 109 German ships seized in internment in American harbours. Mechanics performed remarkable repair jobs on these liners after their German crews had done their best to destroy the engines. Admiral Sims' first job was to send thirty-four destroyers to Queenstown

*Above:* 'We are here, Lafayette!'. The Rainbow Division marches into St Nazaire in November 1917. *Below:* Brigadier-General Douglas MacArthur with the Prince of Wales in France

(now Cóbh – Cork, Ireland). Reinforcements of American destroyers on convoy and anti-submarine duty, based at Queenstown, Brest and Gibraltar, helped to cut Allied shipping losses by nearly two-thirds by November 1917. About half the American soldiers were landed at British ports, mostly Liverpool and Glasgow, proceeding to France in a cross-channel fleet of small converted transports. The other half were landed at South-Atlantic French ports, usually Brest. The U-Boat commanders never seriously endangered the passage of the AEF to Europe; but the *Tuscania* and *Moldavia* carrying men of the 32nd and 4th Divisions were torpedoed off the English coast in February and May 1918 resulting in a loss of 169 lives.

**Admiral William S Sims**

The *Persic* was also sunk on 9th September, but the passengers and crew were taken aboard British destroyers.

As the days shortened and autumn winds blew cold, the arrival of the American army on French soil clearly brought a much-needed uplift to French morale. Throughout 1917 there was hardly a sector from the North Sea to Verdun that was not severely engaged in battle. Great hopes for an Allied breakthrough in the Spring and yet another offensive in Italy on the Isonzo were now submerged in the swamps of Passchendaele and the waters of the Piave. Nivelle's great French onslaught in April east and west of Reims had resulted in complete failure. Although the British had achieved early success at Vimy Ridge and had taken the brunt of the fighting after the French defeat in April, Haig failed to capture the German U-Boat bases on the Belgian coast and the Ypres offensive had ended with November stalemate.

Depression caused by Nivelle's defeat and mutinous demonstrations in no less than sixteen French army corps hung like a pall over France. Against this chaotic background General Pershing's eyes turned eastwards from Paris to select a suitable theatre of operations for the American Expeditionary Force. The British army, guarding the Channel ports essential to their lines of communication, were committed to operations in Flanders, Artois and Picardy. The French were most concerned with that portion of the line defending Paris. The region Neufchâteau – Nancy – Epinal in Lorraine south-east of Verdun between the Meuse in the west and just across the Moselle at Nancy in the north-east suggested a logical location for a training area. Moreover, due north in the same province the fortified area of Metz, protecting German lines of communication with northern France and valuable captured coal and iron fields, offered a strategical objective of the greatest importance for the American forces.

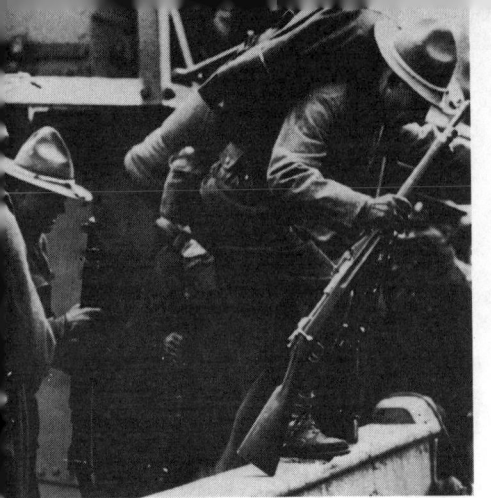

*Left:* The 4th Infantry Regiment disembark at Brest in April 1918. *Right:* German and Austrian troops rest after storming Santa Lucia on the Isonzo sector of the Italian front. *Below:* Stuck in the mud at St Eloi. The British offensive at Ypres in 1917 ended in stalemate by November. *Bottom:* British troops entrain at Poperinghe Gate after the third Battle of Ypres

# Training in Lorraine

The 'doughboys' had barely had time to ask themselves why they were in Europe. 'Why are we here? What do we want?' Gazing from their box cars [thirty-six men or eight horses] as the troop trains steamed eastwards to the forests and green terraced vineyard country of Lorraine, the young soldiers were captivated by the sight of old-world villages and the richly-endowed soil of France. Houses concealed gardens and lawns in the rear hidden from the street. And the girls were so pretty! These troops were not of course the first Americans of the war to be seen in France in uniform. American volunteer flyers were already in action with the Royal Flying Corps and with the crack all-American *Escadrille Lafayette*; American doctors and nurses manned US equipped hospitals and hundreds of drivers were at the wheels of motor ambulances carrying the wounded from casualty clearing stations to base hospitals.

In September 1917 General Pershing established his permanent AEF headquarters in a barracks south-west of the training area at Chaumont on the Marne. The impressive Caserne de Damremont with its tree-lined parade square was the meeting place of many distinguished soldiers, politicians, and civilian guests in the months to come. The essential features of the training plan called for three months of instruction in positional and open warfare, but artillery brigades were trained separately in firing camps assigned by the French for the purpose. As General de Castelnau's zone of command in Lorraine was situated on a quiet sector of the front, instructors from French divisions were released to help train American units on arrival in the area. The 1st Division at full brigade strength in September was already training at Gondrecourt with the crack French 47th Division (*Chasseurs Alpins*). Senior commanders in each division were assigned temporarily as observers in British and French command posts in the line. Fortuitously, during the period of development of the American First Army, the war of attrition on the Western Front in early 1918 at last showed signs of movement. Pershing had no inclination for trench warfare, but envisaged that American troops would enter the passive trenches north of Nancy as part of their training before the year was out.

The mud, rain, snow and long nights of the winter in Lorraine limited the hours of training of the American troops. They were more accustomed to just plain North American frost and snow and heated rooms. Doughboys soaked through with rain on route marches, range or bombing practice dried out in their billets over fires made from green wood cut from the forests. Their inner warmth was preserved when cookhouse meals of canned corned beef hash gave way to ham, bacon, beef and other familiar ingredients of American menus. Few complaints were heard from the regular infantry around Gondrecourt and the 5th Marines at Bourmont, and the National Guardsmen of the Yankee and Rainbow Divisions in camps in the areas of Neufchâteau and Vaucouleurs were just as cheerful.

But eight months had now elapsed since America's declaration of war and the disillusionment of the Supreme War Council with the speed of despatch of American soldiers to Europe was to some extent shared in the winter gloom by the French people. Until his impassioned offer at Clermont-sur-Oise the following Spring of more active support for the Anglo-French armies after Ludendorff's great offensive, both 'Black Jack' Pershing and Tasker Howard Bliss remained obdurate on the question of committing the American Expeditionary Force *en masse* at the front line. A glance at a graph depicting the growth of the AEF in France clearly illustrates nevertheless the impractical nature of British and French demands of the American

**In training in Lorraine**

*Above:* American nurses. *Left:* A Red Cross HQ near the St Mihiel sector. *Below:* General Pershing receives Marshal Foch at Chaumont. *Right:* General Tasker Howard Bliss, recalled from retirement as American Chief of Staff

**Colonel George Patton**

war machine in the winter of 1917. At the conference table of the Supreme War Council at Versailles Pershing and four-star General Bliss – from 6th October the US Army's new Chief-of-Staff – countered the requests of Clemenceau and Lloyd George and their military commanders for immediate reinforcements in the line with stubborn oratory. Thumping the table on one occasion Pershing said: 'Gentlemen, I have thought the programme over very deliberately and will not be coerced.'

The United States was never formally allied with the Entente and Pershing exercised complete jurisdiction over the deployment of his forces until General Foch became Supreme Commander of all Allied Armies after the Beauvais conference in April 1918. Persistent efforts in London and Paris to relieve General Pershing of his command were loyally deflected from President Wilson's attention by Newton D Baker in Washington. A cablegram received by the Secretary of War from Pershing on 8th January emphasised the latter's determination to create a national military identity, and prevent the secondment of his regiments to the French and British, *except* in a real emergency. The Staff officers in the Caserne de Damremont drew cold comfort from the fact that the telephones at Headquarters seldom seemed to work.

The question of armaments and supply – as much as of manpower – was of prime importance. Considering that French and British factories had taken three years to streamline their respective ordnance programmes, the American factories performed a competent feat of organisation in eighteen months or so of war. Of course weapons of war were already being despatched in quantity to many destinations in Europe, and Baruch's economic function was to restrain the wilder urges of commercial enterprise in the national interest. General Pershing, impressed by the record of British marksmanship and stories of 'Limey sharpshooters hitting Boche grenades in flight with rifle fire', ordered thorough range practice for his men in Lorraine. America, since the days of Daniel Boone a nation of crack shots, was the arsenal of good rifles. Each rifleman in upwards of two million men landed in France stepped ashore with his own weapon. It may have been one of the old, dependable 1903 Springfield rifles. More likely it was a modified American-built 1917 Enfield, developed from the British design. Compared with the German Mauser both these .30 calibre rifles – the Enfield also fired Springfield cartridges – were more accurate and of superior speed of fire. Some Krags used in the Spanish-American War and Canadian Ross rifles were in service. The French 8mm Chauchat light automatic rifle was issued, and the excellent .30 light automatic Browning came into use in 1918. German allegations in the Summer of 1918 that American troops were using short barrel or sawn-off shotguns in contravention of the rules of war were undoubtedly true. The shell provided for these guns contained a charge of nine heavy buckshot, a combination of murderous effect in close fighting in the Argonne.

The .45 Colt automatic pistol (Browning 1911) dealt effectively with German bayoneteers; and .45 Colt and Smith Wesson double action revolvers (both 1917) were used similarly in hand-to-hand fighting.

The first of the trench-warfare weapons with which the 'rookie' became acquainted was the hand grenade. The earliest American requirement was for a defensive grenade of the fragmentation type. One American concern turned over from the production of high-grade silverware to furnish these deadly grenades, complete and loaded for shipment overseas. The firing mechanism with its pivoted lever was a radical departure from European practice and thought to make the grenade safer in the hands of the soldier. The infantrymen were also introduced for the first time to offensive, gas and phosphorous grenades. The VB rifle grenade, Mark I, was adapted by American engineers from the French Viven-Bessière type. Of seven different types of trench mortars in Allied use, four were manufactured from the original designs and fired in action. These four were the 3-, 4-, and 6-inch British Newton-Stokes, and the French 240 mm (9.45-inch) mortars. The slightly larger British 11-inch Sutton mortar was also handled by American mortar batteries. The British 8-inch Livens gas projector, Mark II, was adopted and made both in France and America. Electrically-fired and used with devastating effect, the Germans never knew what the cavernous device was that caused such havoc in their ranks. A battalion of the German 52nd Division at Exermont in the Argonne made the acquaintance in October 1918 of 'Edison Gas', a new combination resembling their own 'Yellow Cross' gas. A one-man toxic gas cylinder made in Detroit was not perfected until after the armistice.

Since 1914 the machine-gun had developed into a highly lethal tactical weapon capable of obliterating whole battalions. Typically and historically an American weapon, Gatling brought out the first true machine-gun, which was used in the Civil War and not long after in the Franco-Prussian War. The comparatively light, air-cooled Lewis machine-gun, the invention of another American (Colonel I N Lewis), was a revelation when it came to the aid of the Allies in the early part of the war. Maxim, Lewis and Colt guns were in evidence on the Mexican border, but when the first AEF contingent set sail they had only a few of the French Benét-Mercié guns on board. Machine-gun battalions of the first twelve American divisions in France were equipped with the French army 8mm Hotchkiss, an air-cooled, heavy machine-gun with an impressive record dating from the beginning of the war. The Hotchkiss was soon joined in the field by the heavy, mobile American .30 Vickers (1915) and the .30 Colt (1917); but the efforts of the ordnance factories in 1917 were turned mainly towards the production of Browning and Lewis guns. America's greatest feat in machine-gun production can be attributed to the inventive genius of John M Browning, who had been associated with the history of rapid fire guns and automatic weapons ever since he had patented the breech-loading rifle in 1879 when aged twenty-four.

The 1917 water-cooled Browning Heavy was developed alongside a synchronized aircraft version of the rigid type, a tank model (not completed until 1919) and the .30 light automatic machine rifle; but troops did not receive either the machine gun or the rifle until June 1918. In fact the Browning Heavy was first severely tested in the Argonne-Meuse offensive. The Browning, more than a match for enemy Spandaus and Maxims, was an unqualified success in the battle. The guns were often used for overhead fire, and during the advance one company fired 10,000 rounds per gun into the Ogons Wood on the Kriemhilde Line. Although the guns were externally rusted after the Atlantic voyage and ammunition belts covered in mud, the gunners were not unduly hindered by stoppages.

Great strides were made in the First World War in the concentration and distribution of artillery fire in selected target areas. The advent of the artillery board enabled command posts to plot zero lines and swiftly correct ranging shots from information given by officers dangerously located in ground and aerial observation posts. Furthermore, with the permanent record of targets plotted on these grid sheets the full fury of gunner batteries was brought accurately to bear upon the enemy within a matter of minutes. The reputation of Schneider et Cie and the glorious record of French gunners in action naturally prompted the US army to look to France for artillery equipment and modern gunnery instruction. Gun crews were introduced principally to the 75mm field gun (the famous *soixante-quinze*) and the 155mm howitzer and companion GPF gun by English-speaking French instructors, nobly assisted by French-speaking Americans and French-Canadians with the help of hastily translated training manuals. American factories however successfully adapted and duplicated many French and British mobile guns; and in 1918 an assortment of models from the calibre 75mm Schneider (and the adapted American 3-inch version of the same gun) to the French and American-built 240mm howitzer and its near rival in specification the British 9.2-inch howitzer were supplied to the Western Front before the end of hostilities.

America's own contribution, the 4.7-inch field gun (1906), could – with the trail depressed into a hole in the ground – send a 46-lb shell just over six miles, and was employed at closer range to knock out German 75mms. In the first scramble to unearth all available weapons, small numbers of the rather old, heavy 5-inch and 6-inch howitzers with ranges of nine and ten miles respectively were borrowed from American Coast artillery sites and naval ordnance and sent to France with suitable mountings. Last in the category of mobile field guns assigned to almost all US artillery brigades were the British 8-inch and 9.2-inch and French 240mm howitzers. For fighting the aeroplane improvised 75mm anti-aircraft guns were mounted on trucks, and the Americans developed their own high-powered 3-inch gun, which was mounted on a four-wheel trailer of the motor type. Heavy machine-guns were also mounted on trailers for the main purpose of air defence.

In 1917 practically all field artillery was of the horse-drawn type; but mid-1918 saw the arrival of $2\frac{1}{2}$-ton to 20-ton caterpillar artillery tractors and self-propelled caterpillar gun mounts and trailers; accompanied by four-wheel-drive trucks for hauling ammunition and equipment for repairs. In the field of transport generally American officers borrowed precious horses, wagons, carts, bicycles and assorted motor vehicles from the French and British; but in 1918, in addition to supplying great numbers of mules, horses and horse-drawn vehicles, the United States sent supplies of passenger cars, motor-cycles, motor ambulances and $1\frac{1}{2}$-ton to 5-ton motor trucks adapted to suit the various needs of combat and supply. Although the American factories turned enthusiastically to the production of two kinds of tank based on the French two-man Renault and the larger British type, hardly any were despatched from North America before the armistice. The United States, however, supplied the power plant and driving details for a big Anglo-American tank (Mark VIII), which was assembled by engineers in France. Major George S Patton, the first recruit to the US Tank Corps, set up the first American tank training school in France and commanded the 1st Tank Brigade at St Mihiel and in the Argonne. Manpower was always given the priority over equipment and food supplies on

The US .45-inch Model 1911A1 automatic pistol. This became the standard US Army pistol in 1926, and has remained in service to this day, nearly 2½ million examples of the type having been manufactured. The A1 differs only very slightly from its First World War predecessor, the Model 1911, also made by Colt (and by Remington under licence). The chief exterior differences of the A1 are a shorter, serrated trigger, an arched main spring housing (at the bottom rear of the stock) and a wider foresight. *Calibre:* .45-inch. *Operation:* Recoil, automatic. *Length overall:* 8.62 inches. *Length of barrel:* 5 inches. *Feed:* Detachable box magazine holding seven rounds. *Weight:* 2.43lbs. *Muzzle velocity:* 830 feet per second

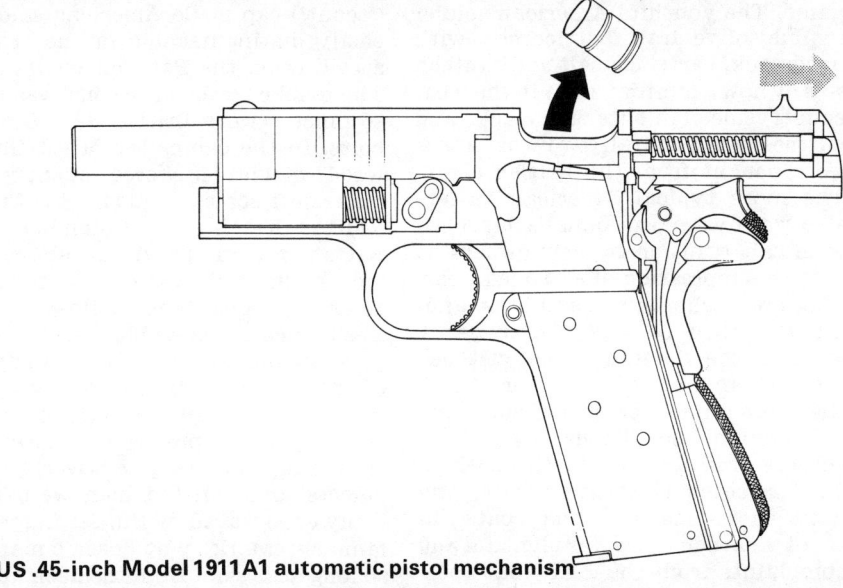

The US .45-inch Model 1911A1 automatic pistol mechanism

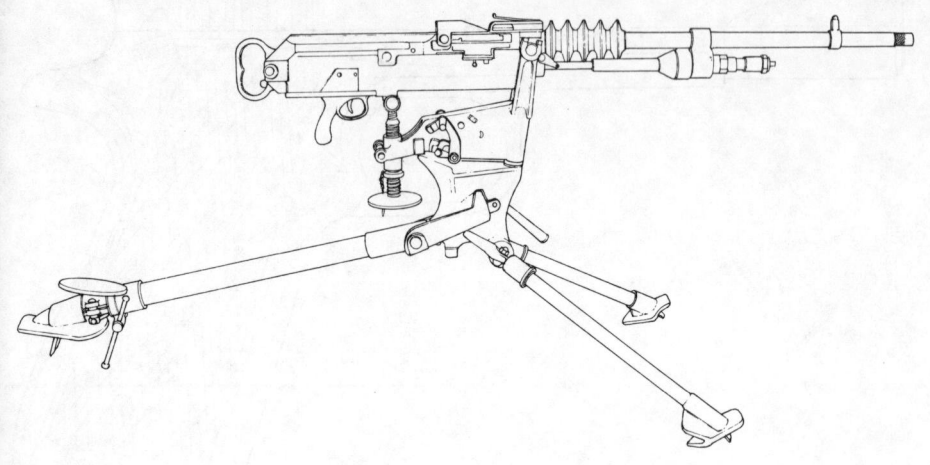

the Atlantic sea lanes; if it was a question of room for men or horses, then the horses were left behind.

When the bugle called 'halt' on the march in Lorraine and exhausted gun crews unhitched horse from limber after a day on the firing range, talk was reminiscent of chatter at the ball game. The youthful American soldier in his olive-drab battledress with haversack, cartridge belt and canteen was by now a familiar sight in the local countryside. Tin hats, gas masks and puttees worn spirally to the knees were bought from the British army. The more typical American gaiters also worn were occasionally bleached with salt solution by new owners to give the impression of seasoned wear. Shoes were short-lived and the manufacturers had to apply three heavy soles to the Pershing shoe, stitched screwed and nailed together before the shoes stood a chance of surviving the rough conditions underfoot. Officers trailing mud in the path of duty rejected their greatcoats, and wore short-length trench coats instead. Leave in Paris was plentiful and complaints from the AEF that their troops looked poor cousins to the smartly-dressed soldiers in Europe led to tunics being cut so slim that men at all mindful of sartorial elegance were prevented from putting fountain pens in inside pockets. Breeches were replaced by long trousers and the melton cloth, overseas ('scout') cap made American soldiers easily distinguishable in the crowds strolling on the Parisian boulevards. The market price of leather was high so officers wore British Sam Browne belts. In the camps the latest Hollywood movies flickered silently on makeshift screens and the Red Cross, YMCA, Knights of Columbus and Salvation Army provided welfare services. The daily rations based on a generous subsistence allowance of fresh meat, vegetables and white bread included a welcome daily supply of free cigarettes, pipe tobacco and candy. Water and American coffee with meals were preferred to the *vin du pays* and *café au lait*. Over-weight officers and enlisted men were probably encouraged by Hunter Liggett's famous remark: 'Fat doesn't matter, so long as it's not from the neck up!'

The French 8mm Hotchkiss M1916 machine gun (on a 1916 tripod). This was the basic French medium machine gun of the First World War. It was an air-cooled weapon, and though somewhat heavy for such a gun, was reliable and well-liked by its users. The shortage of machine guns in US divisions in France led to twelve of them being equipped with Hotchkiss machine guns, a total of 5,255 being bought by the United States. Most were converted to .30-06 calibre. *Calibre:* 8mm. *Operation:* Gas. *Length overall:* 51.6 inches. *Length of barrel:* 31 inches. *Weight of gun:* 55.7lbs. *Weight of tripod:* 60lbs. *Feed:* Strips containing 24 or 30 rounds, or a 250-round belt made up of strips joined together. *Muzzle velocity:* 2,325 feet per second. *Cyclic rate of fire:* 450 to 500 rounds per minute

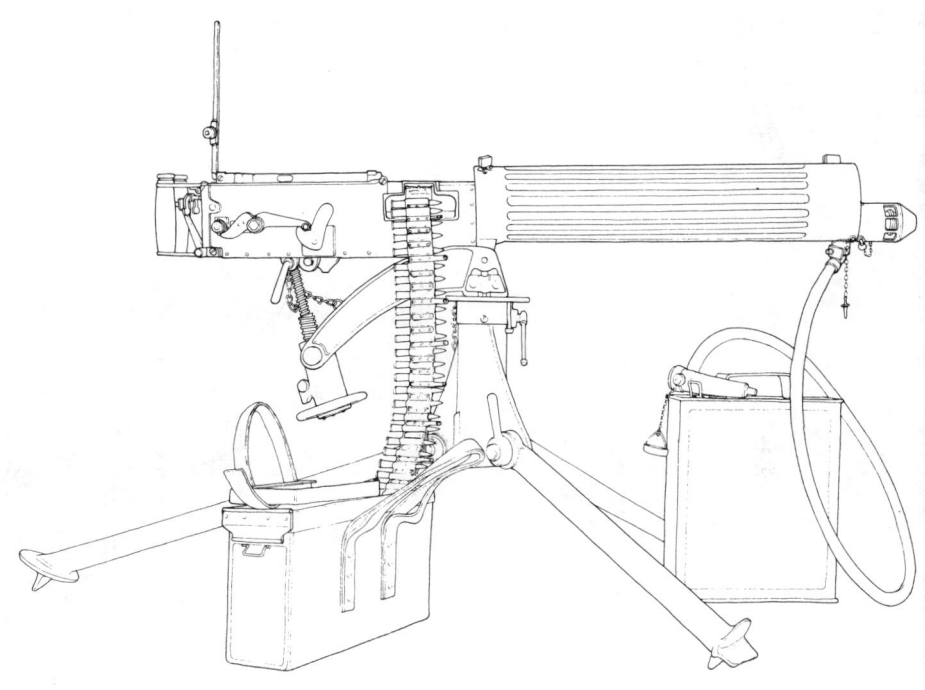

The British Vickers .303-inch Machine Gun Mark I (on Mark IVB tripod). This was Britain's basic infantry machine gun in both world wars, and though heavy, it proved its worth by its sheer ruggedness and reliability. It was adopted, as the Vickers Maxim, in 1912. *Calibre:* .303-inch. *Operation:* Recoil, with gas boost from the muzzle booster. *Weight:* 33lbs (40 with water). *Weight of tripod:* 50lbs. *Length overall:* 43 inches. *Length of barrel:* 28.4 inches. *Feed:* Canvas belt holding 250 rounds. *Muzzle velocity:* 2,440 feet per second. *Cyclic rate of fire:* 450 to 550 rounds per minute

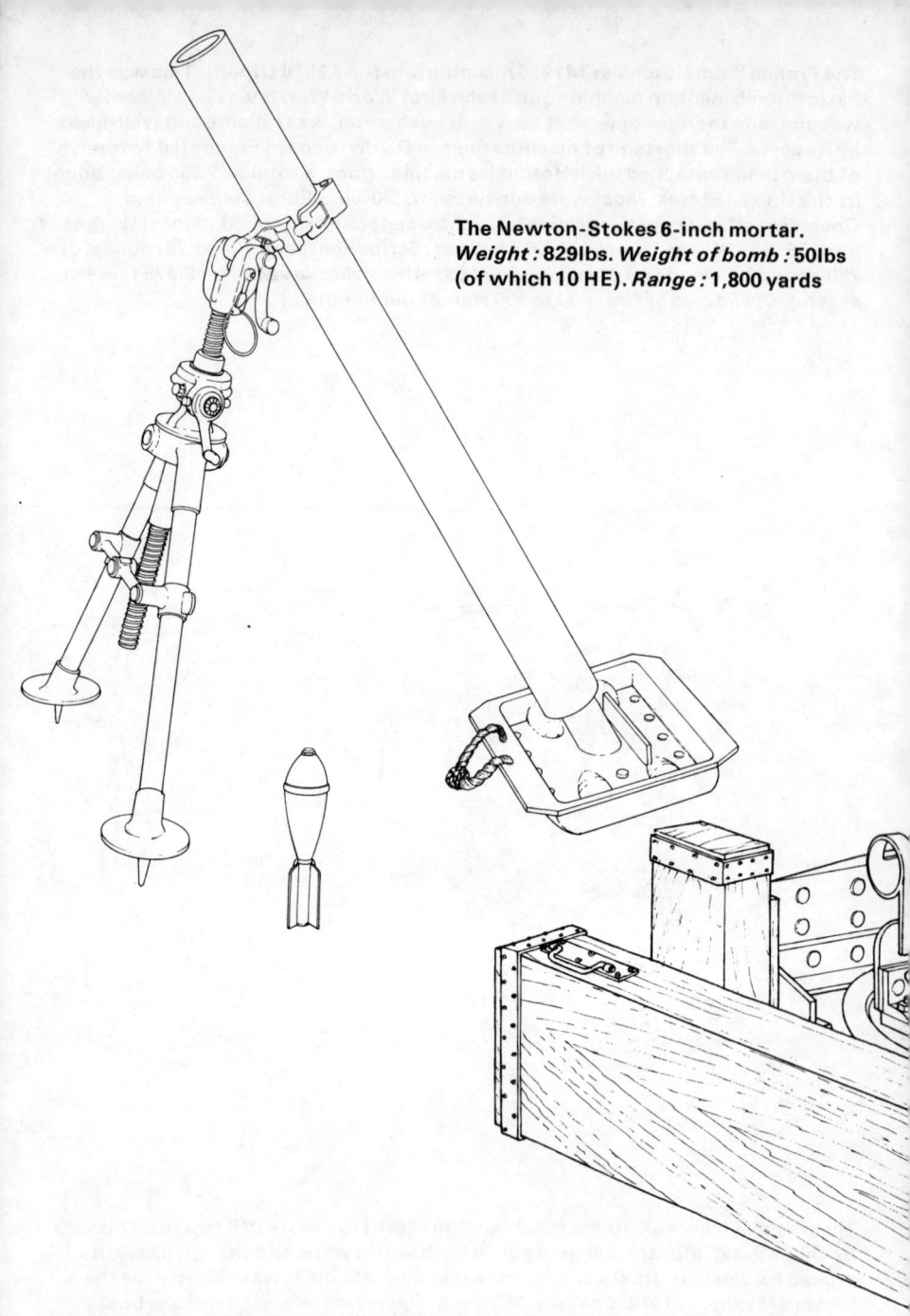

**The Newton-Stokes 6-inch mortar.** *Weight:* 829lbs. *Weight of bomb:* 50lbs (of which 10 HE). *Range:* 1,800 yards

**The French 240mm mortar.** *Weight:* 3,700lbs. *Weight of bomb:* 195.8lbs (of which 90 HE) or 120lbs (of which 60 HE). *Range:* 2,200 yards with 195.8lb bomb or 3,100 yards with 120lb bomb

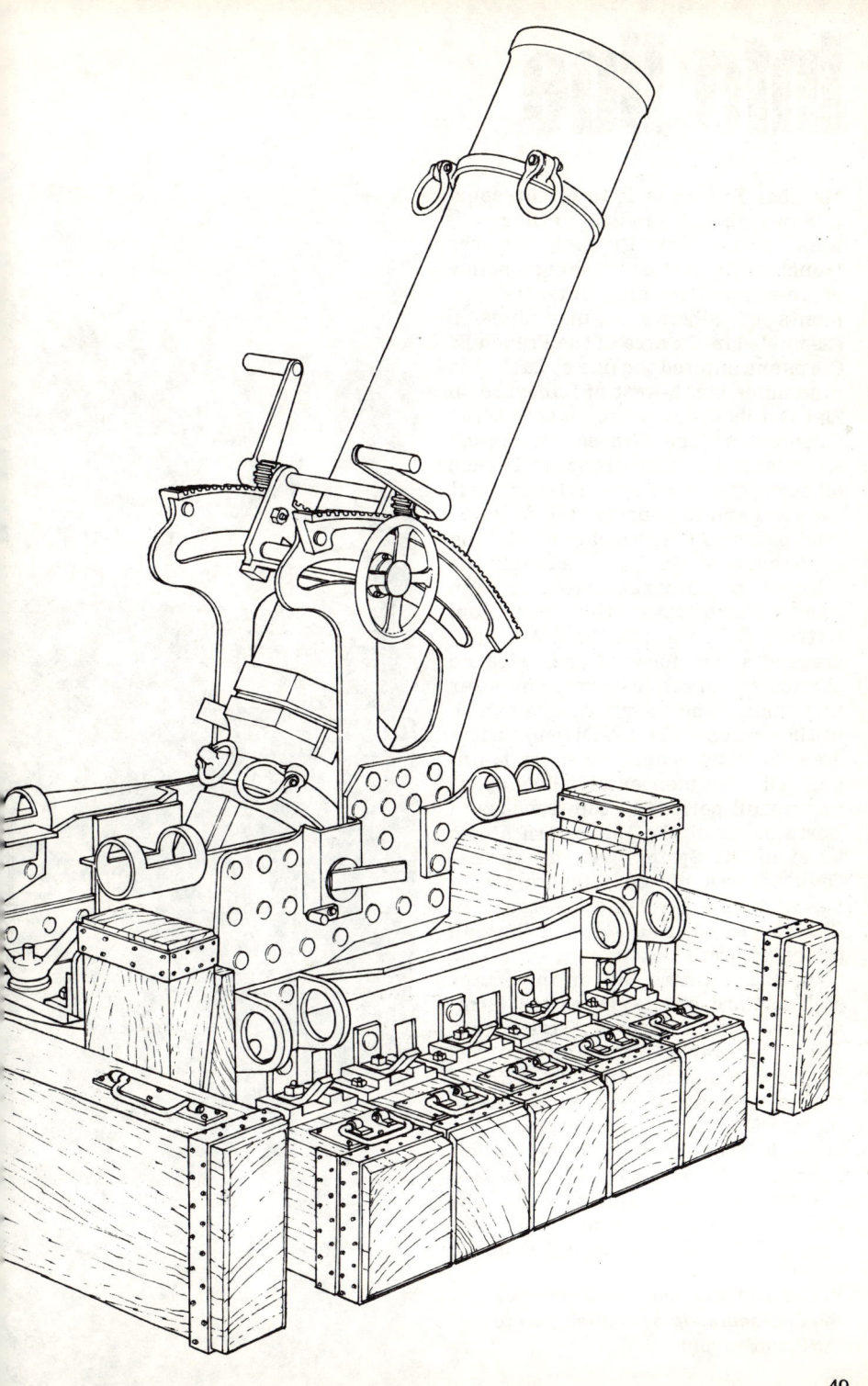

# Into line

Marshal Joffre's visit to Gondrecourt in September 1917 indicated the readiness of the 1st Division for the trenches. As part of Pershing's policy of in-school training, infantry elements of Sibert's regular division assembled in the area of the French IX Corps and entered the line by battalion nine miles north-west of Lunéville on 21st October, gunner regiments being dispersed at the disposal of French sector artillery. Chaperoned by French officers, the marching infantry left the road and in pouring rain followed mud paths to the trenches stretching a distance of six miles between the villages of Bezange-la-Grande and Parroy. Two days later men from Battery C of the 6th Field Artillery dragged a gun forward and, with no particular target in view, sent their first shell at the enemy. After a month in the trenches the 1st Division withdrew to Gondrecourt for more training. All four pioneer divisions spent uneventful periods in the trenches in Lorraine until the Ludendorff storm burst in the Spring, but the Yankee Division was moved temporarily to the Chemin-des-Dames sector in Champagne where batches of German prisoners were taken.

On 26th January 1918 an important step forward was taken in the formation of the American First Army. Major-General Hunter Liggett was named Commander of I Corps AEF. In normal circumstances a corps was to include four combat, one replacement and one depot division. The movement overseas of the 1st, 26th and 42nd Divisions had been concluded, and the 2nd, 32nd (replacement) and 41st (depot) Divisions were at full strength

**British and American soldiers watch the *Chasseurs Alpins* on their way to the Picardy front**

by the end of March. Brigadier-General William G Haan's 32nd Division, recruited from the National Guard of Michigan and Wisconsin, made Liggett's I Corps complete. Some of the first draft men had found their way into the 26th and 32nd Divisions. The regular 3rd (Major-General Joseph T Dickman) and 93rd (Provisional) Divisions disembarked in March and concentrated at Château-villain and Bar-sur-Seine. Brigadier-General Roy Hoffman's 'provisional' division consisted of four negro combat regiments of National Guardsmen, three of which were in fact formally attached to the French Fourth Army west of the Argonne. The fourth – the 370th Infantry Regiment – performed an itinerant role under French direction in Lorraine and participated in the Oise – Aisne operation in September 1918. Major-General John E McMahon's 5th Division (Regular Army), supplemented by draftees, commenced training with the French in Lorraine on 1st June. We have noted that since January the Germans had been watching the build-up of American forces in France with concern; but if after the Beauvais conference General Foch knew that the trump card was more or less under his control, he was never slow to rudely remind General Pershing that his arm was still too weak to play it in major offensive action.

After observing the role played by aircraft in the Spring offensive, Major William ('Billy') Mitchell, US Signal Corps, a keen flyer with a two-year-old logbook, conferred with Major-General Sir Hugh M Trenchard. Trenchard, then commanding the newly-designated Royal Air Force, told him he was convinced that the aeroplane was an offensive and not a defensive weapon. Both Trenchard and Bishop, who submitted a detailed plan to Pershing for the organisation of the AEF Air Service, were destined to be principal architects of the foundation of modern air power. Having first launched a craft in powered flight, America had played little attention to the development of military machines. No American-built plane carried a machine-gun or bomb-dropping apparatus in 1917. The 1st Aero Squadron with 'pusher' biplanes – mostly Curtiss

*Left:* German troops on the Chemin des Dames. *Above:* General William ('Billy') Mitchell

J2s – was indifferently employed in Mexico; on declaration of war the US army had only fifty-five combat machines, and in Pershing's view fifty-one were obsolete and four obsolescent. The French Premier, Ribot, asked for 4,500 American planes, 5,000 pilots and 50,000 mechanics; but visions of a 'cloud of planes' hovering like locusts over Berlin were unfulfilled. The Allies had not previously turned to America for aircraft on the same scale as they had for munitions, and factories were not prepared for production in quantity. In 1917 the Air Service, since 1907 the responsibility of the Chief Signal Officer, had 131 pilots and no specific policy. The Foulois draft production programme provided for 22,625 aircraft, almost 44,000 engines, plus eighty per cent spares (equalling the guts of another 17,600 aircraft); in the words of Chief Signal Officer Squier, 'an army in the air of winged cavalry on gas-driven flying horses'. In reality some 3,000 planes covered the AEF's zones of advance, although only about 750 were American-built. Major Bishop, advancing in rank to Brigadier-General, commanded the Air Service of I Corps, First Army and First Army Group. Pershing made Brigadier-General Mason M Patrick Chief of Air Service in Spring 1918 and Brigadier-General Benjamin D Foulois was the first Commander of Air Service First Army with Mitchell as his deputy.

Forty-five American squadrons were airborne by the end of the war; twelve of these squadrons being equipped with American-built planes and Liberty engines. The squadrons were tactically allocated to either pursuit, observation or bombing roles. Cadets came after primary flying training in the United States and Canada for advanced training in Europe. The principal Air Service school was at Issoudon near Bourges in central France where, if lack of facilities at first enforced unwelcome drill and cookhouse fatigues, at $100 a month the 'Million Dollar Guard' could afford to alleviate boredom in a carefree manner. 767 pilots qualified for wings under French, British and American instructors. As a result of Major Raynal C Bolling's mission to the front in June 1917, it was soon decided

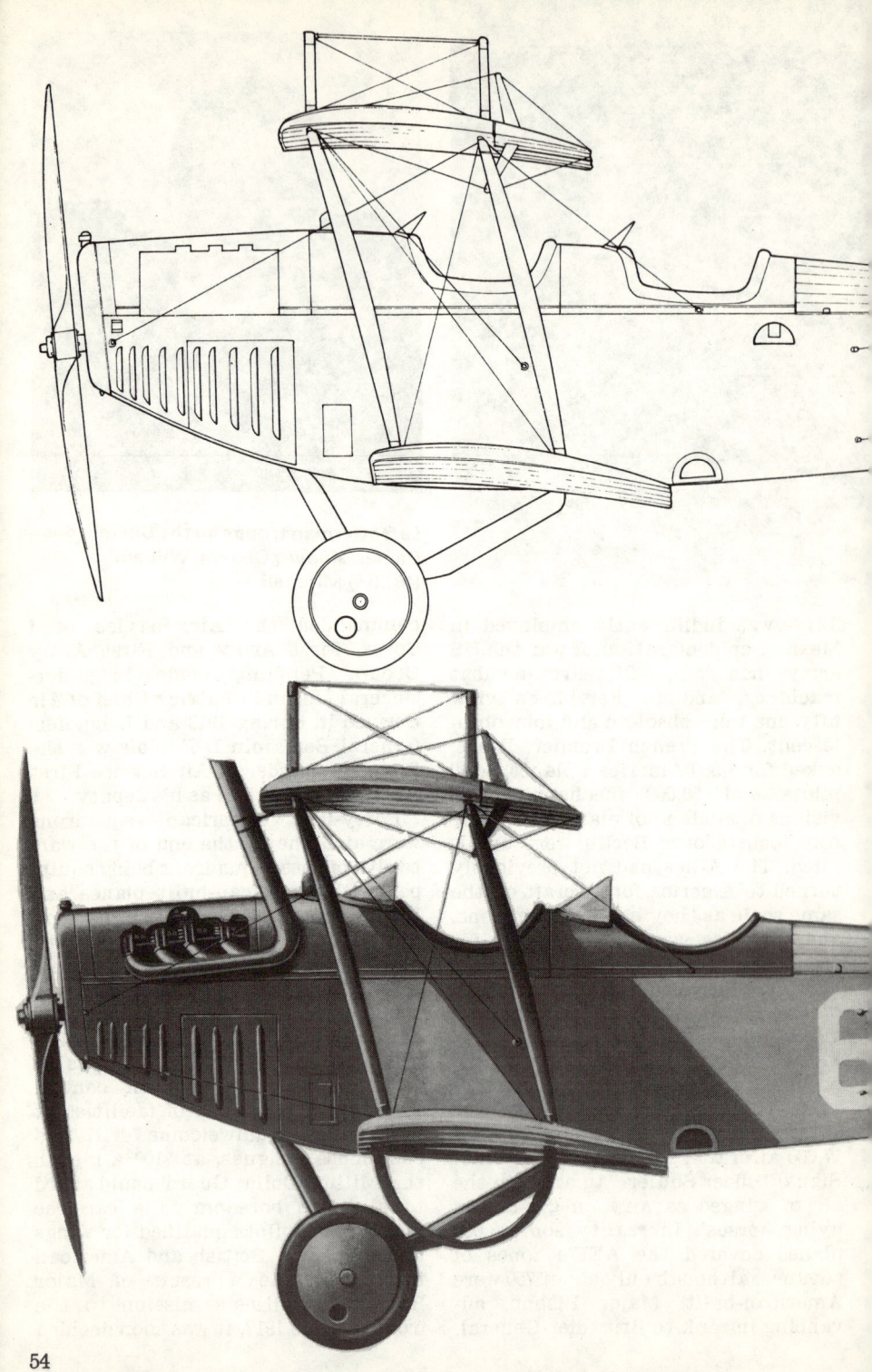

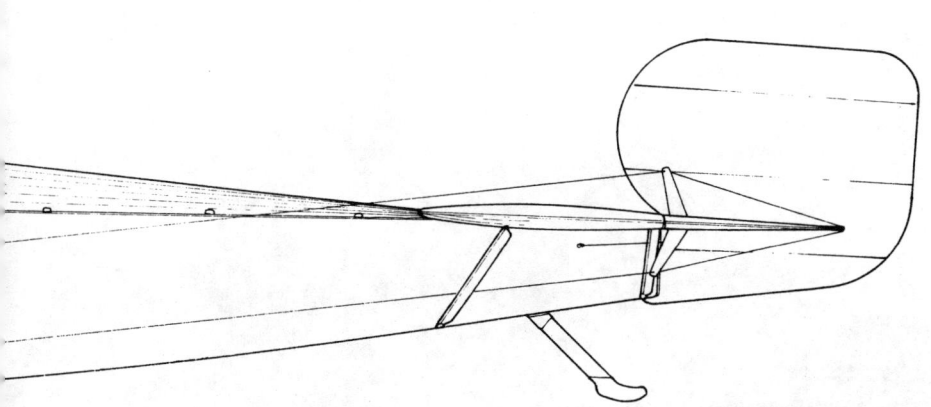

The Curtiss JN-2. This trainer was the precursor of the JN-4, which resembled it in every important respect except the means of controlling the aircraft. The JN-2 was fitted with the so-called 'Deperdussin' type of controls, in which the control column was fitted with a wheel, movement of the wheel working the rudder, and that of the column in the fore and aft direction the elevators. Lateral control was worked by a yoke fitted to the pilot's shoulders. The JN-4 had the more common system whereby elevators and ailerons were operated by the control column, and the rudder by the rudder bar

The Curtiss JN-4 'Jenny'. This primary trainer was derived from the earlier JN-2, and first appeared in 1916. It was a good trainer, docile and safe, but sensitive enough to give aspiring pilots every advantage in their training. *Engine:* One Curtiss OX-5, 90hp. *Speed:* 75mph. *Climb:* 10 minutes to 2,000 feet. *Ceiling:* 11,000 feet. *Endurance:* 2 hours 18 minutes. *Weight empty/loaded:* 1,580/2,130lbs. *Span:* 43 feet $7\frac{1}{8}$ inches. *Length:* 27 feet 4 inches

*Above:* Raoul Lufbery, French-born American air ace
*Below:* Lieutenant Edward Rickenbacker, America's top-ranking ace with 26 victories. *Right:* Major Carl 'Tooey' Spaatz, a young squadron commander and future Commanding General of the United States Army Air Force

that the best course was to concentrate on the design and construction of training aircraft and buy fighter aircraft from the Allies. 'Pusher types' had now been almost replaced in aviation development by 'tractor-type' aircraft. The Curtiss JN ('Jenny') trainers and in particular the JN4D compared favourably with the Avro 504 of the Royal Flying Corps but the powerful Liberty engine used also in varying cylinder capacity in modified French, British and Italian aircraft was the most outstanding achievement of wartime American industry.

The 1st Aero Squadron from Columbus, New Mexico, was the first American flying unit to reach Europe in September 1917. The Escadrille Lafayette formed the nucleus of 103rd Pursuit Squadron, and veteran American combat pilots did not at first take kindly to the new boys. Those who volunteered to fight for the French had overcome the problem of nationality by enlisting in the French Foreign Legion. One of the earliest recruits was French-born Raoul Lufbery, who had been recognized as an ace since 1916, and ranked third in the final roll of American ace pilots. In March 1918 the 94th and 95th Pursuit Squadrons were located in the zone of advance, but unfortunately the Nieuports that equipped these squadrons were without machine-guns. When this omission was rectified, it was learned that the pilots of 95th Squadron had received no gunnery instruction. This gave the 94th, the famous 'Hat-in-the-Ring' Squadron, the honour of being the first American outfit to go into combat on 3rd April. Eleven days later Lieutenants Alan F Winslow and Douglas Campbell scored their first victories when they shot down two German aircraft.

The camera played an important role in the sphere of aerial reconnaissance towards the end of the war. As observation planes had been forced to fly at greater altitudes by enemy ground defences, cameras were de-

*Above:* 'Kite' balloon. *Below:* German troops in retreat on the Chemin des Dames sector of the Soissons offensive

veloped to operate in conditions of increased range, speed and vibration. With longer focus lenses, special dry plates and colour filters, paths newly-made by a party of infantrymen and wheel tracks in soft ground could be defined from an altitude of four miles. 100,000 prints were made from negatives freshly taken in the last four days of the Argonne – Meuse offensive. In 1916 wireless telegraphy from plane to base was accomplished up to a range of 140 miles, and messages were successfully telegraphed between planes in flight. In February 1917 the voice was first crudely transmitted from plane to ground by radio telephone. Realising the potential of voice communication for ground and combat control, the US Signal Corps overtook French and British experiments in producing a plane radio telephone set. The first combined transmitting and receiving sets powered by light dynamos were turned out in the USA well ahead of the delivery of the planes in which they were to be used. The range was purposely limited to two or three miles for obvious security reasons. The radio telephone was a great help to artillery spotters perched in 'kite' balloons as well.

The difficulty of swiftly communicating target references by wireless telegraphy and visual signals from aircraft early in the war had led to the introduction of captive 'kite' balloons at the front. The hydrogen-filled balloon, a familiar aspect of static air defence in Britain in the Second World War and still used by British paratroopers for practice parachute descents, was controlled by windlass and cable from a mobile truck. Supported by 37,500 cubic feet of hydrogen contained in a gas bag made of rubberized cloth, two artillery officers slung in the observation basket could, on a fine day, comfortably observe activity on the ground from an altitude of up to 5,000 feet over a radius of ten miles or more. From the beginning communication with the ground was mostly made by telephone line dropped over the side of the basket. Clearly a hazardous assignment for the spotters: the life of a captive balloon at the front was reckoned to be fifteen days; and German airmen rated balloon-busting as being worth $1\frac{1}{2}$ planes per balloon for the record. When balloons were destroyed spotters made good their escape by parachute. A parachute basket-device in which the escapees descended with salvaged equipment was also in use. US artillery brigades were equipped with some 500 balloons of American manufacture. Observers were known to make four escapes on a busy day and in the Argonne thirty balloon jumps were made by American soldiers.

Three weeks after Pershing offered Pétain his experienced divisions at Clermont-sur-Oise, the 1st Division was ordered to a billeting area at Gisors north-west of Paris. After Ludendorff's offensive on the Somme (Operation George) the line southeast of Amiens extended through the area of Montdidier; and the German First and Seventh Armies were grouped before the Chemin-des-Dames for the advance on the line Soissons – Reims. On the night of 24th April the 1st Division took station at Froissy in the area of French VI Corps (French First Army), and the 1st Infantry Brigade (Hines) was inserted between the French 45th and 165th Divisions in the Cantigny sector, three miles west of Montdidier. The objective assigned to the American regulars was to relieve pressure on the British on the Montdidier heights by capturing the small town of Cantigny. Reconnaissance and raiding began immediately from both sides, and German gunners aloft on the hill at Cantigny hurled a constant barrage of 8-inch shells at American batteries, and at infantry crouching in scattered rifle pits. On 25th May the 2nd Infantry Brigade (Buck) started digging jumping-off trenches, and in the early hours of the 28th Summerall's Brigade artillery commenced ranging fire on the German hill position. Men of the 26th and 28th Infantry, assisted by Stokes mortars, 37mm cannon and machine-gunners of the 1st Brigade, moved forward from the brown earth in unison with the artillery timetable. Spurning their battledress tunics, the men advanced in shirtsleeves each carrying 220 rounds of rifle ammunition, two hand grenades, a rifle grenade and enough food and water for two days. Platoon commanders hardly needed maps in the darkness, as they had studied their assignments so thoroughly. The bold frontal attack on Cantigny was conducted just like another practice exercise at Gondrecourt. The shelling from Summerall's 75mm and 155mm guns ceased, and during the day the 2nd Brigade took the town, which lay in ruins around the château. The first major engagement of the American war was over for the loss of 100 men and 350 prisoners.

But while Bullard's 1st Division was digging in at Cantigny, the news from

*Below:* The first serious American casualties at Cantigny. *Right:* American casualties from the Oise-Aisne battles arrive at the Gare du Nord in Paris. *Below right:* German troops cross the wreckage of a bridge on the Aisne canal

the Marne was far from good. After saturating the Chemin-des-Dames with shell, mortar bomb and gas, the Crown Prince's Operation 'Blücher' in Champagne crossed the Aisne and the Vesle on 27th May, and in three days advanced through the hilly, wooded country of the Marne valley to Château Thierry. Another Battle of the Marne? The Germans on the road to Paris again? On 29th May Dickman's 3rd Division entrained at village stations in Lorraine for the Marne river, although the track from Châlons to Epernay along the north bank was not in use. A motorized machine-gun battalion of this division encountered hordes of refugees and crowded ambulances on roads leading southwards from the battle area. The 5th and 6th Infantry Brigades (Sladen and Crawford) were dispersed east and west of Château Thierry amongst the French 20th, 4th Cavalry and 10th Colonial Divisions. General Dickman possessed no artillery at this time. On 1st June the regular infantry and marines of Bundy's 2nd Division were given to the French XXI Corps, and placed in a second line position along a thirteen-mile front astride the road from Château Thierry to Paris. Bundy's artillery was delayed by rail chaos, but the 3rd Infantry and 4th Marine Brigades (Lewis and Harbord) manned the vital sector across the road the same night. The motorized machine-gunners were quickly in action covering French engineers blowing the river bridge; and were joined in their defensive position on the south bank by machine-gunners of the Marine Brigade, who arrived exhausted in the area after marching some fifty miles. Meanwhile fierce fighting had developed in the neighbourhood of Villers - Cotterêts on Bundy's left flank.

By taking Hill 204 overlooking the Paris road, German observers held a commanding view of French and American positions south and west of the river. German planes buzzed overhead, and observation balloons flecked the sky over the north bank. The 4th Marine Brigade on the left flank faced the Belleau and Bouresches woods seven miles north-west of Château Thierry; the regular 3rd Infantry Brigade being on its right from Bonneil to well across the Paris road. Repulsing a German attack on the 4th, Harbord's marines advanced on 6th June through rock-strewn ground cut with ravines and thick undergrowth to straighten the line in the direction of Torcy. A few bursts of artillery fire straddled the wood, and concentrated all too briefly on Bouresches about a mile to the south-east. Both wooded areas and the village of Bouresches were infested with machine-gun nests and rifle posts defended by veteran German soldiers. In the

words of contemporary author Barrie Pitt: 'The weather was perfect – heat haze, dancing midges, gentle breezes . . . Five yards apart, in four ranks, twenty yards between each rank the marines advanced. Nothing had been seen like it, in mass innocence, in hope and at the end in unavailing heroism and self-sacrifice, since the British attack on the Somme in 1916 . . . For nearly a hundred yards the marines walked forwards in silence . . . Then with the sharp crack of a thousand snapping sticks the hidden machine-guns opened fire . . .' As the marines stumbled on Belleau Wood, demands for Stokes mortar support from hitherto silent officers mingled with urgent cries for stretcher bearers.

Trapped in interlocking fields of fire, advancing troops were exposed to enemy machine-guns at a range of fifty feet in dense thicket. Dropping their packs, shirts open and rifles in hand, the marines put all faith in their bayonets as they closed on the German gunners. At the onset of the attack on Bouresches village, a battalion commander – who swore vehemently at a man in uniform standing in full view of the enemy – was to learn that he had rebuked the chaplain. On the second day the cellars of the small village were cleared of every German in hiding and a young officer rashly drove down the village street in a motor car; but the battle in Belleau

**An artist's impression of the battle for Belleau Wood**

Wood raged for nineteen days. The marines in the southern part of Belleau Wood and Bouresches were fiercely bombarded and 'Yperite' (mustard) gas clung to the earth and trees. Part of the 3rd Brigade and 7th Infantry of the 3rd Division were sent to Belleau before the wood was captured by the Americans after such desperate struggle on 25th June; Major Shearer, commanding the 3rd Battalion of the 5th Marines, reporting 'This wood now exclusively US Marine Corps'. Bewildered German prisoners said that they had been briefed to expect an unruly, ill-trained American mob and they were greatly surprised by their determination. Altogether 700 Germans were taken in the fighting; but the 4th Marine Brigade suffered 5,711 casualties and lost half its officers.

The 2nd Division south and west of the Marne was in constant action throughout the month of June. As part of the Brigade assault on 6th June, three companies of the 3rd Battalion successfully attacked Hill 142 and drove northwards towards the Lucy-Torcy road. When the 49th Company reached its objective on the north slope of the hill, Sergeant Hoffman saw twelve of the enemy, armed with light machine-guns, crawling towards his group. Giving the alarm, he bayoneted the two leaders and forced the others to drop their guns and run, the Germans being obliged to abandon a position from which they could have swept the hill with machine-gun fire. Sergeant Hoffman of Brooklyn, New York, was awarded the first Congressional Medal of Honor of the war. Advancing on Vaux and nearby positions along the line to Hill 204, the 3rd Brigade took the village on 1st July; having first demolished all the houses with large cellars with pinpoint artillery fire.

The first crossing of Böhn's Seventh Army at Château Thierry was hindered by the machine-gun fire of Dickman's 3rd Division; but the Germans did cross the Marne about six miles further east with the intention of cutting rail communication between Paris and Epernay. The 3rd Division was involved in local actions in this area until, on 15th July, Ludendorff made the supreme effort (Operation *Friedenssturm*) with three armies concentrating twenty miles further east towards Epernay and Châlons. The 26th (Yankee) Division, which had returned in April from the Chemin-des-Dames sector to Lorraine, now relieved the 2nd Division in the devastated areas of Belleau, Bouresches and Vaux. The 1st Division at Cantigny to the left of the Montdidier-Noyon defence line was alerted by the bombardment of 'Operation *Gneisenau*' on 9th June; but did not engage in the action of the French First and Third Armies, and just over a month later moved under French XX Corps to relieve the 1st Moroccan Division south-west of Soissons.

The exploits of the Marine Corps at the gateway to Paris caught the imagination of the French people. The fighting spirit and apparent contempt for death of American troops in action made a deep impression on allies as well as on the enemy. During 1918 French womenfolk confessed that they cried more for Americans leaving for the front than over their own battle-hardened men. 'They were so young, looked so innocent and were so far from home.' By the end of July twenty-seven complete US divisions were in France and elements of another ten divisions were also on French soil. The Franco-American counteroffensive of 18th July followed three days after Ludendorff's assault on the Marne river line; in fifteen days the Germans were expelled from the Aisne-Marne salient, and Marshal Foch resolved to launch the victory offensive in the autumn.

**French colonial troops in a front line trench**

# The Aisne-Marne counter-offensive

*Left:* A German officer mans a Maxim gun in the Second Battle of the Marne. *Above:* A French 75mm (the *soixante-quinze*) in action near Reims. *Below:* US negro troops attached to Gouraud's Fourth Army west of the Argonne Forest. *Bottom:* The ruins of Château-Thierry, deserted by the Germans

Foch was not taken by surprise on the Marne on 15th July. Planes and agents had reported vast ammunition dumps, and heavy concentrations of men and artillery appearing in Champagne; and German prisoners who talked under interrogation gave General Gouraud's Fourth Army east of Reims seven hours notice of the assault. When Ludendorff advanced east and west of Reims, his first objectives were the capture of the famous cathedral city and a decisive blow at the gateway to Paris. From Château Thierry in the west to the Argonne Forest in the east, the Crown Prince's Group of thirty-nine divisions were on the attack. Menoher's 42nd Division, which had received a liberal dose of gas in the quiet eastern Baccarat sector, was assigned with some Coast artillery units to French Fourth Army Command in the Espérance and Souain sectors of IV and XXI Corps. (The three negro US infantry regiments in service with Fourth Army were highly praised by General Gouraud.) The Rainbows fiercely engaged enemy batteries with their 155mm guns, and trained their 75mms with open sights on waves of advancing infantry. One infantry company held six successive attacks with steady rifle and machine-gun fire. On the Château Thierry front heavy-calibre shells fell into the 2nd Division area on villages adjacent to bridges, railway lines and important roads.

But it was Dickman's day on 15th July. The regular 3rd Division faced three German divisions crossing the river, covered by the fire of 500 batteries. The Germans advanced rapidly and overran the Paris – Châlons track and the 3rd, under French III Corps, could do little but slow them down. Refused permission to counterattack

**An American officer engages a German plane near Soissons**

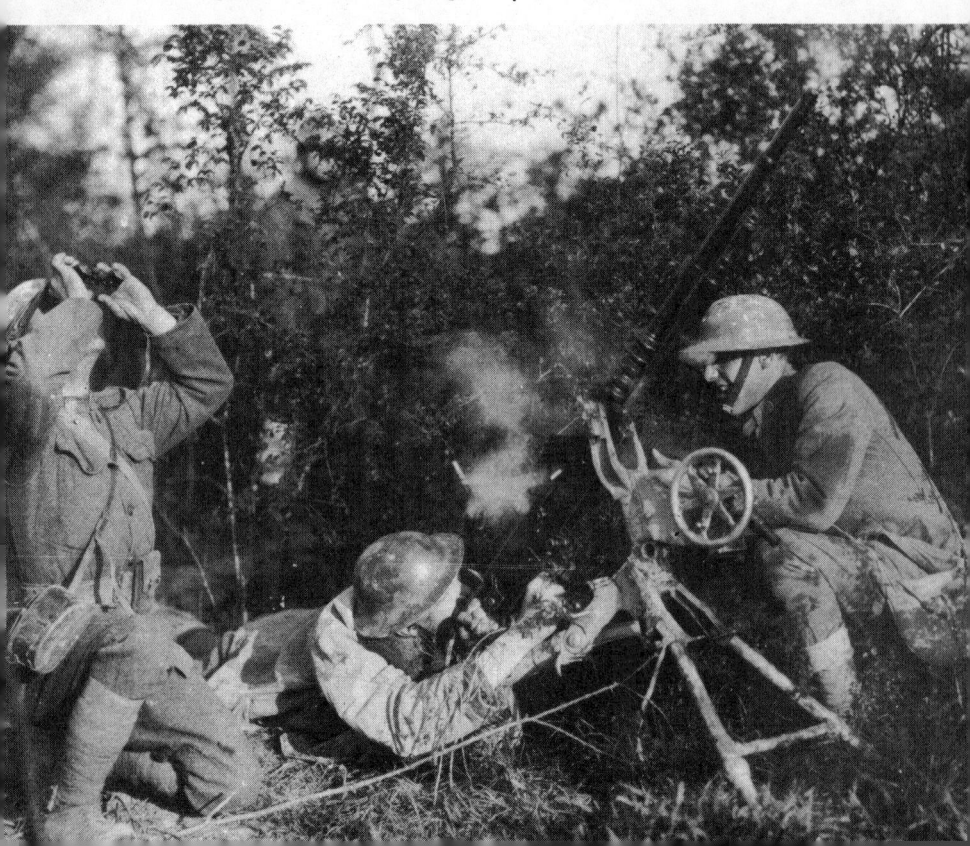

by his Corps commander, General Dickman's reply was prompt: '... but the American flag has been forced to retire. This is unendurable ... humiliating to us and unacceptable to our country's honor. We are going to counterattack.' The following day the 3rd Division held its ground on the Fozzoy – Crézancy road. McAlexander's 38th Infantry ('The Rock of the Marne') in fact prevented the crossing of some units and threw the German 10th and 36th Divisions into complete confusion, capturing 600 prisoners. The men of this regiment contained the crossing on its own front, firing on the small bridgehead from three sides, while on either flank the Germans who had gained a foothold pressed forward. The companion 30th Infantry Regiment (Butts) of 6th Infantry Brigade sustained the heaviest attack on the Corps front however, and earned a warm citation from General Pétain in Orders of the Army. The French stood fast on the Montagne de Reims: further east the attacks of Mudra and Einem towards Châlons failed in the face of Gouraud's determined resistance; but Böhn made every effort to push his divisions in the bridgehead towards Epernay to interrupt traffic between that town and the city of Reims. Franco-American counterblows halted his progress; and on 19th/20th July Böhn finally pulled back from below the Marne.

According to Chancellor von Hertling, the history of the world was played out in the first three days of the Aisne – Marne counteroffensive, and even the most optimistic German leaders knew then their cause was lost. Pétain's orders from Foch were to collapse the bulge protruding from the line Soissons – Reims by driving in strength at the base of the salient at Soissons. The pincer movement on the western sector (sometimes called the Soissons offensive) was conducted by Mangin and Degoutte's Tenth and Sixth Armies and initiated from the Retz Forest (Villers – Cotterêts) in the north and from the Marne in the south opposite Château Thierry. The capture of Soissons would lead to the recovery of the Heights of the Aisne. In the east the Soissons offensive was supported by Berthelot's Fifth and Gouraud's Fourth Armies on the attack on either side of Reims. The story of the drive on the western curve of the salient is one of intense rivalry between French and American divisions as they stormed forward to the Aisne without mercy for Ludendorff's faltering army. In the thickly wooded terrain over which they fought, deep, boulder-strewn ravines and thick undergrowth traversed their paths; and in the heat of summer crops matured in rich farmland. The woods, villages, and stone-built farm compounds were all fortified with artillery and machine guns. Hills held commanding views of each line of approach, and a good system of roads facilitated the supply and movement of the German defenders.

West of Château Thierry, Clarence R Edward's 26th Division, which had engaged German storm troops at Seicheprey during two hard months on the Toul sector, captured Belleau village and Torcy and went on north-eastwards to the Ourcq. In between the French 39th and 167th Divisions the Yankees strayed from their pivotal position in the line and drove the Germans from Hill 193 under heavy machine-gun fire. Emulating the example of the German engineers, the 3rd, 28th (Keystone) and 42nd Divisions scrambled across the Marne under heavy bombardment on 21st July on pontoon bridges. The town of Château Thierry then yielded to Dickman's 3rd Division, which had played such an heroic role in the defence of the south bank of the river. By this time the Germans knew that they must retire from the southern portion of the salient. Back from Hill 193 to rejoin their proper route, the 26th's advance through Trugny Wood and Epieds ran obliquely parallel to the

Ludendorff inspects pilots of Baron von Richthofen's pursuit flight. The 'Red Baron's' Albatros biplane stands in the background

3rd Division's approach from Château Thierry to Jaulgonne and Ronchères. On the night of 25th July Menoher's 42nd Division – with Douglas MacArthur as Chief-of-Staff – passed through the Yankee Division in the Forest of Fère near Croix Rouge Farm. This typical French farm compound was built with thick, stone walls and mortar capable of withstanding machine-gun fire. After six hours of reconnaissance work, a battalion of the 42nd found a ditch alongside a road running from the southern entrance to the farm. The capture of Croix Rouge farm, which opened the way for the 42nd to the Heights of the Ourcq, was effected when leading companies emerged silently from the ditch and rushed the farm on the one side that was unprotected.

In between Menoher and Dickman, Muir's 28th (Keystone) Division, less Weigel's 56th Infantry Brigade under French 73rd Division, leap-frogged from the Marne to meet hidden enemy batteries east of Sergy in the Meunière Wood. Weigel's Brigade in fact operated with the Yankee Division as far as the Forest of Fère. Darrah's 55th Brigade was to prove its worth in gallantry between Sergy and Ronchères on the banks of the Ourcq, where the river – usually fordable – was swollen by heavy rain.

On 27th July the whole Allied line from Baslieux near Reims to Bruyères near Soissons straightened out; and on the Ourcq the progress of the

American divisions from the Marne meant an advance of fourteen miles on a front about five miles broad. On 30th July after fifteen days of continual action Dickman's 3rd Division was relieved at Ronchères by Haan's 32nd Division from Alsace. On the left the Rainbows, under shell fire and strafing by the bright red planes of the late Baron von Richthofen's squadron, met face-to-face with the defenders rallied by the 4th Prussian Guard on the Heights of the Ourcq at Fère-en-Tardenois. Any doubts that the Germans would resist on the Ourcq were answered by the severity of the hand-to-hand fighting. On the right – with the Keystone Division also retired – Haan's 32nd, which was not originally a combat division, was caught in long-range gunfire and lacerated with machine-gun enfilade at every step of the advance from Ronchères Wood. West of Coulanges the Rainbows, a battalion of which had taken three days to subdue Muercy farm, was replaced by Cameron's regular 4th Division, which had already seen action on 18th July at the south-eastern edge of the Retz Forest in liaison with the French 33rd and 44th Divisions.

Between the Ourcq and the Vesle, which flows into the Aisne a few miles east of Soissons, the 4th and 32nd Divisions met with still more fortress obstacles in the villages, farmhouses and woods. Hill 230 and Planchette Wood fell on 1st August. The intensity of the hand-to-hand combat was illustrated at Planchette Wood by a line of ten dead American riflemen lying opposite ten dead German riflemen. Their bayonet contest had ended when the last few men left standing were hit by a burst from a machine-gun. On 2nd August General Mangin's capture of Soissons at last made Reims secure, and on the approach march to the Vesle the Germans were seen to be withdrawing. Engineers, cooks and clerks were ordered up to stretch their legs in general pursuit of Ludendorff's army retreating across the Vesle to the Aisne. The 4th and 32nd encountered three days of very stiff fighting in the valley of the Vesle, but the 32nd crowned the week's work by clearing the river town of Fismes of machine-gun posts and snipers by 6th August. Recalled to the battle, the 28th Division – relieving the 4th – charged across a broken bridge and occupied Fismettes on the north bank of the river. As the French Sixth Army attacked German positions between the Vesle and the Aisne, the line was extended eastwards of Soissons to the Oise. As part of the Oise – Aisne operation, Duncan's 77th Division — replacing the 32nd – plunged into crucibles of fire in the Vesle bridgeheads at Château du Diable and Bazoches. The hell's kitchen of Château du Diable was not reduced until 22nd August. The Paris — Verdun track (between Soissons and Fismes) was clear. A week later Böhn's Seventh Army continued its withdrawal to prepared positions north of the Aisne.

The directive from GHQ, Western Front, of 4th August stated that the American First Army would in principle comprise two army corps,

**A German patrol sees Soissons in the distance**

placed side by side with four US divisions in the first line. In fact on that date Liggett's I Corps north of the Marne contained one US and one French division in the first line with one American division in each of the second and third lines. On III Corps' front on the right Bullard likewise had the French 4th amongst his four combat divisions. Whereas when Bullard relieved French XXXVIII Corps on Liggett's right on the Vesle, the American First Army did not *per se* comprise a national group, the change brought two American corps side by side for the first time on a World War battle front. Orders issued from Chaumont announcing the organisation of the American First Army on 24th July were made effective on 10th August.

With I, II (on the British sector) and III Corps in the line, 'Black Jack' Pershing with 1,500,000 men on the payroll was given the quiet sector on the Woëvre, extending from Nomeny (east of the Moselle) to a point south of St Mihiel for the assembly of his reserve and training divisions. The Vesle sector was promptly handed back to the French Sixth Army and the American First Army was concentrated on the St Mihiel front.

The principles of a September offensive had been discussed at the Chaumont conference in July; but with victory on the Marne and better still the pride of the British army restored on the Somme, Marshal Foch was encouraged on 30th August to travel to First Army Headquarters at Ligny-en-Barrois to meet General Pershing. Foch outlined his plans for a concentric movement against the enemy. He proposed that while the British and the French left hammered the Siegfried Position, the French on right of centre together with the American forces – after the reduction of the St Mihiel salient – should push along the Meuse and attack towards Mézières in the Ardennes. General Pershing rightly assumed the Marshal's plan mean another dispersal of American forces under French command. The general suggested that the United States be given the entire sector from the Meuse to the Argonne Forest. He declared, moreover, that he was prepared to raise a second American army *west* of the Argonne, only to be accused by Foch of procrastination.

Pershing submitted his plans in writing to Foch for the St Mihiel operation, and an all-American offensive in the Argonne. The atmosphere was more cordial at Foch's headquarters on 2nd September when Pétain and Pershing were called to discuss the future operations of American forces. The St Mihiel attack would take place about 10th September. Marshal Foch said that in his opinion the American army would not be ready to attack west of the Meuse until the third week in September. The Argonne – Meuse offensive would be executed by the American army with all available divisions about 20th-25th September. Prior to the attack General Pershing would take over command of the front from the present right of the American First Army, at Port-sur-Seille, westwards to include the Argonne Forest, approximately ninety miles. This directive of course gave the American army lines of advance west and east of the Meuse, and accepted, once and for all, the assignment of a distinct American theatre of operations. As General Pershing drew up his final arrangements for the St Mihiel battle a few days hence, he decided to give command of the First Army after the first phase in the Argonne to his senior corps commander, General Hunter Liggett. At the same time the end of St Mihiel would allow the American Second Army to assemble east of the Meuse. General Robert L Bullard – the first divisional commander to land in France – was to be given the command of the Second Army, assigned to a secondary covering role advancing across the plain of the Woëvre towards Metz.

*Above:* US munitions convoy on the St Mihiel front. *Below:* General Pershing inspects his troops

# The way to the Argonne

General Pershing's lack of Army reserves or auxiliary troops was a direct result of French demands for trained combat troops. Priority in the transport ships was given to fighting personnel, and supplies of food and equipment were often sacrificed in favour of manpower for the front. In spite of this, the American Services of Supply (SOS) had grown prodigiously in the spring and summer months of 1918. Over 7,000,000 tons of supplies were ferried across the Atlantic and deposited in storage depots in the base, intermediate and advanced zones of war. In addition to augmenting the military needs of the Allies, American engineers, working on rail tracks and roadways, contributed in no small measure to the economic rehabilitation of the French nation. New shipping berths, warehouses and depots were constructed in principal port facilities at St Nazaire, La Pallice, Marseilles and Brest. American navy blue thronged the long lines of quays; mechanical cranes were installed and stevedores worked energetically to achieve a swift turn round in shipping. Inland the American Expeditionary Force was everywhere – drilling, building, planning and forwarding supplies: cutting wood from the forests; repairing roads, laying new telephone lines. Base hospitals existed now at St Nazaire, Bazoilles, Dijon and Bordeaux. In August surgeons in these main hospitals and in American Red Cross tented hospitals were at work

**German prisoners in St Mihiel after the salient collapsed in September**

*Above:* A pontoon bridge built by American engineers at St Mihiel. *Above right:* American engineers clear away wire entanglements from an old German position to make way for a new road to the front. *Below:* American soldiers with a French tank

dealing with some 50,000 American casualties brought in by hospital trains from the Marne. American nurses and women welfare workers of the Army Medical Corps and Red Cross tended the needs of the sick and wounded.

The French railway system was inadequate. Thousands of miles of railway track ranging from the standard broad gauge down to the narrow 60cm track were laid down right through to No-Man's Land. Apart from armoured and hospital trains, the United States supplied locomotives and freight cars for the transportation of ordnance, rations and baled hay for the animals. Engineers built storage, arrival and departure yards, warehouse tracks, engine terminals, water points and repair shops. They opened quarries and collected debris from ruined villages and shattered farm houses to repair shell-blasted roadways. Pontoons, which had changed little in design since the Civil War, and sectional steel bridges surmounted river obstacles; wood trestles traversed wide mine craters. The sappers made mines and booby traps inoperative and counter-mined roads and paths in the battle areas. Corduroy and brush paths through the forests enabled the guns to be towed across thick undergrowth. Combatant engineers, who many times dropped their tools and seized rifles in the heat of action, were employed filling in trenches and removing wire entanglements. They cut their way through barbed-wire entrenchments to engage machine-gun posts with Bangalore torpedoes. In engine shops mechanics repaired tanks and put power plant and driving details into new chassis. In the Argonne the engineers took their tool bags and repairs forward to keep the tanks moving.

Pershing's plan to break the St Mihiel salient – sixteen miles at its deepest point – envisaged a drive in greatest strength in the west and east at the Haudioment – Pont-à-Mousson base line. In the battle for Lorraine in 1914 the Germans had fastened on to the natural, wooded ramparts of the Meuse heights, which formed part of the salient and held fast. The concrete Michel Position now backed the base of the salient on the edge of the Woëvre plain. In the west the heights formed a wall to the salient, woods and villages lay cloistered on the rear slopes. In the east a patchwork of ridges and small hills rose amongst more villages, lakes, ponds and clumps of trees. St Mihiel itself was situated at the face of the salient near the river Meuse. A few miles east of St Mihiel, Mont sec enjoyed a commanding view and, although the

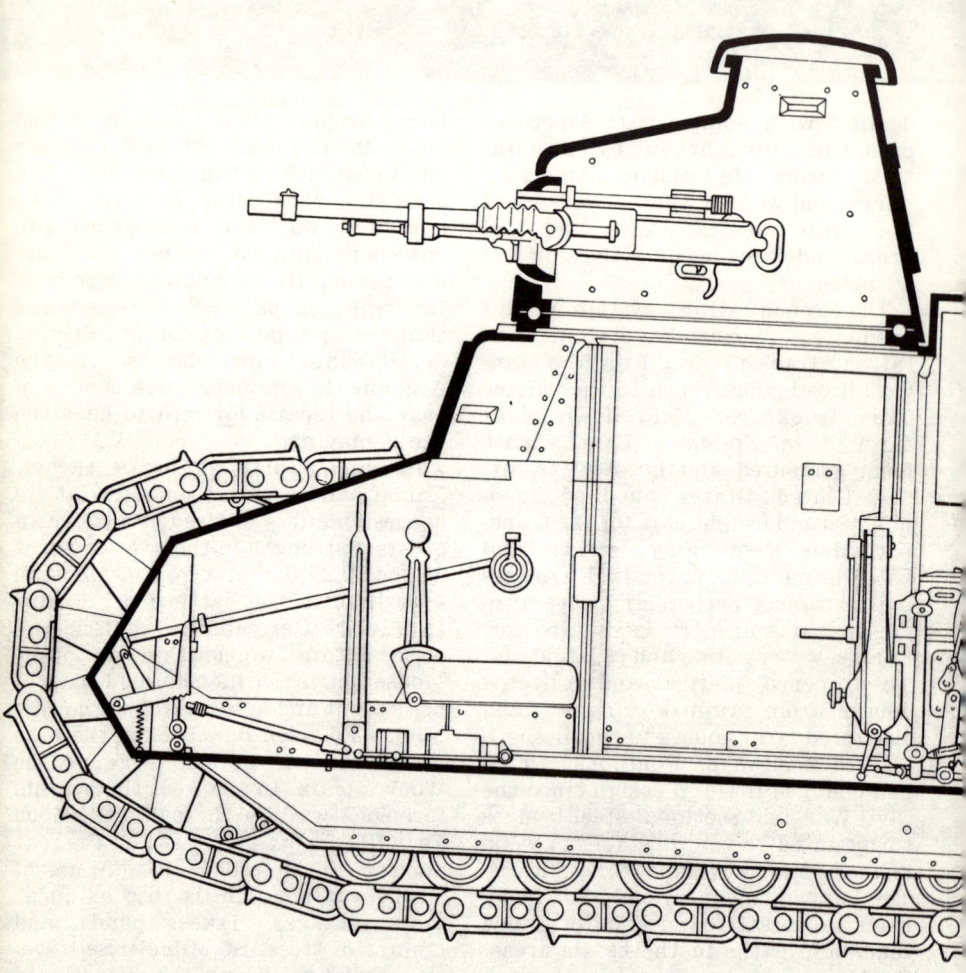

The French Renault FT 17 light tank. This was the most successful French tank of the First World War, and remained in service into the Second. The cast turret had a 360-degree traverse, and could mount an 8mm machine gun, a 37mm cannon or a 75mm gun. There was no chassis as such, equipment being attached onto the hull directly. This helped to save considerable weight, as did the fact that the main part of the track idler wheels was of wood. The FT 17 suffered in its cross country performance from having only a short length of track on the ground, so a detachable 'tail' was provided. This helped the vehicle make its way out of shell holes and over trenches. *Weight:* 6.9 tons. *Crew:* 2. *Armament:* One 8mm Hotchkiss machine gun with 4,800 rounds. *Armour:* 16mm hull nose, driver's plate, sides and rear, turret front, sides and mantlet; 8mm glacis plate, engine covers, turret roof and cupola; and 6mm hull decking and belly. *Engine:* Renault 4-cyclinder, 35hp. *Speed:* 4.74mph on road, 1.5mph cross-country. *Range:* 22 miles on roads, 12.5 miles cross country. *Fording:* 2 feet 3.5 inches. *Trench:* 5 feet 9 inches. *Step:* 2 feet. *Length:* 16 feet 5 inches. *Width:* 5 feet 8.5 inches. *Height:* 7 feet 0.25 inch

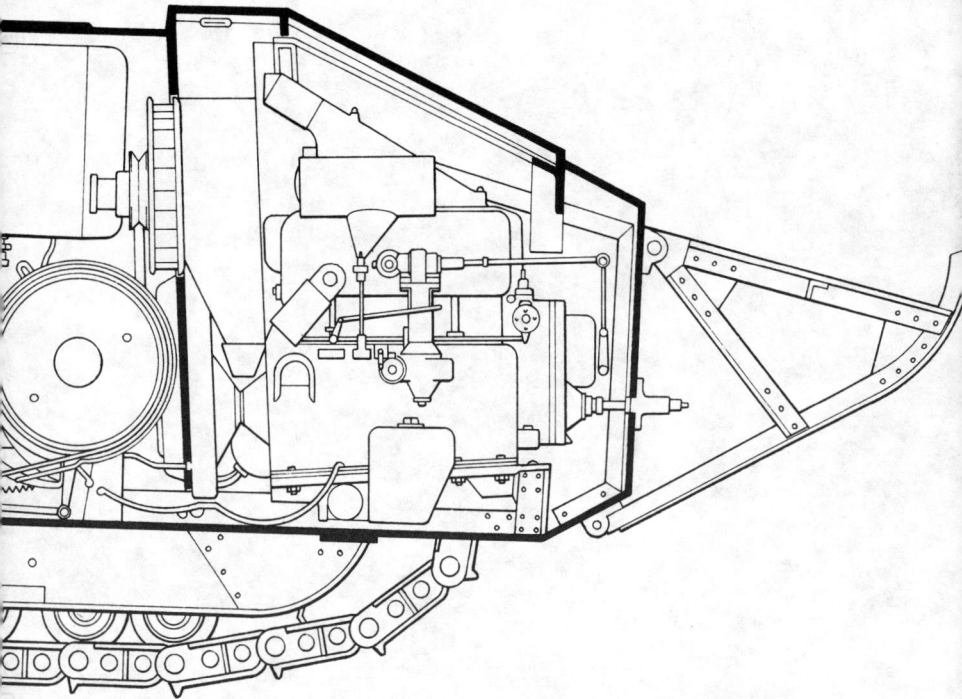

Germans were gradually pulling out, all the high ground was strongly defended and three or four lines of barbed wire impeded access to the open country.

Pershing's artillery, heavily augmented from Allied reserves, opened up at 0530 hours on 12th September. An hour later yellow flares went up in the daylight and the infantry went over the top. In the west Cameron's V Corps, including one French division, struck eastwards from the high ground not far south of Verdun. In the centre French Colonial II Corps edged forward at the nose of the salient. In the south and east between Seicheprey and the Moselle the seven American divisions of I and IV Corps went northwards towards the Michel Position. Patton's Tank Brigade and French tanks trundled ahead of the infantry across roads, fields, trenches and ditches looking for machine-gun nests.

Detailed plans for the strategic withdrawal of Fuch's Army Unit C to the Michel Position were scrapped in favour of *ad hoc* measures for swift escape. The attack came at what General von Ledebur, Chief-of-Staff, termed 'the most unfavourable moment imaginable'. The Germans had formed a good opinion of the quality of American troops when the 26th (Yankee) Division was in action at

Seicheprey prior to the Marne battle. American prisoners looked well fed, strong individuals, doubtless possessing military potentialities. The Germans had nine divisions in the salient; but some of these were made up from reserves. Stoutly defending the hills, the German army was deployed in three separate groups. German batteries, with guns sited in deep echelon, hit back strongly at American and French gun positions, advancing tanks and infantry. The events of 12th September are highlighted by the race – won at nightfall by the Yankee Division – between the 26th from the west and the 1st Division from the east to Vigneulles at the centre of the Haudioment – Pont-à-Mousson line. The next day Fuchs ordered his forces, which included two Saxonian, a *Landwehr* and an Austrian division, back to the protection of the Michel Position. The American First Army took 15,000 prisoners and 200 guns. The capture of the Verdun – Avricourt section of railway track, following the clearance around Soissons, made the rail-link between Paris and the Lorraine border complete. When stragglers were not pursued north of Vigneulles General

**Grim-faced American prisoners, taken in the Argonne, stand with their German captors**

von Gallwitz of *Heeresgruppe Gallwitz* in Lorraine, who was quite aware of General Pershing's commitments along the Meuse, immediately alerted von der Marwitz's Fifth Army near Verdun.

Gallwitz assessed in August that there were twenty-eight American divisions in France. They attacked effectively, but always in cooperation with French forces. His calculations were assisted by interrogation soured when they were not escorted safely back to their planes. The arrival of the American First Army at St Mihiel confirmed Gallwitz's belief that General Pershing's goal was the independent assignment of his forces with specific objectives. An attack from St Mihiel across the plain of the Woëvre appeared at first to be a likely course of action. Indeed American officers expected that an investment of Metz in Spring 1919

reports on American pilots, who on occasion made flights behind the lines to meet the Kaiser's army in person. On being asked why they were in France, they usually confessed that they had not grasped the political implications, but America certainly did not seek influence in Europe. Allied complaints of the transgressors were best pacified by withdrawal with honour to the Fatherland. The friendliness of the airmen was unhappily would lead to the American army's advance to the Rhine as the right arm of the victory offensive. Gallwitz was uncertain if Foch was aware that the Metz Fortress was almost stripped of its guns; but the German army group commander attached greater importance to blocking the route to the Briey-Longwy Iron Basin – a principal source of German armaments – and the rail-link in the supply line from Metz and Diedenhofen [Thionville] by way of Longuyon to the north-west.

In the last stages of mobile warfare in 1914 the iron chain drawn across France from the North Sea ended a few miles east of Verdun at St Mihiel. The troublesome salient, which finds no reference in the Schlieffen Plan, is more correctly viewed as the sharp end of the Alsace – Lorraine stalemate. Twenty-three miles west of the city of Verdun, the natural bulwark of the Argonne performed a similar pivotal function on the opposing defence lines to the man-made bastion of the forts of Verdun. On the one side lay the Western Front and on the other a passive 'Eastern Front' stretching to the Swiss Border.

The Argonne Forest, a natural barrier between Champagne and Lorraine, is aligned south-east to north-west between the Aisne and the Aire, and runs almost parallel to the course of the Meuse. The western slope of the ridge is traced by the river line of the Aisne, and the eastern boundary is marked by steep cliffs. This conspicuously wooded ridge is about ten miles broad, it rises to an average height of 1,150 feet, and stretches a distance of forty-four miles. The northern extremity of the Argonne Forest is marked by the Bourgogne Wood, which lies opposite across the valley to the Woëvre Forest on the Heights of the Meuse. The southern

**General Max von Gallwitz (third left, front row), commander of the German army group north of Verdun**

tip is situated twenty miles south-west of Verdun in the neighbourhood of Brizeaux. The military value of the Argonne can largely be attributed to the Aire and its tributaries, which dissect the high ground into deep valleys. The only lateral road gap runs between St Menehould and Clermont

The 'Liberty' Division in action with rifle grenades in the Argonne Forest

on the Châlons – Verdun highway. Even if the forest were stripped bare of its pine trees, the ridge – cut by ravines and hills – presents a formidable barrier to the invader. Heights of every shape from sharp ridges and rounded hills to peaked summits are crowned by woods. Tongues of woods run across valleys. Patches of woods and thicket cover ravines and gullies. High ground leads to still higher ground with concealed crests. Unlike the more usual European forest locale – easy of access with open ground – undergrowth grows freely. For the Americans the Argonne Forest was the Indian country of the primeval Adirondacks.

The Argonne is also defined as a much bigger area – sixty-three miles deep by twenty miles broad, connecting the plateaux of the Haute-Marne and the Ardennes, and bounded in the west by the Ante and Aisne and in the east by the Meuse. Between the eastern boundary of the Argonne Forest to the north and the Meuse river the breadth of the valley varies from between ten and twelve miles; but north-west of Verdun mass movement through the valley is barred by a triangular group of heights. Gaps do of course exist: a railway track and road follow the Aire through the western gap at Fléville; another road crosses longitudinally between the Heights of Romagne and Cunel; and a main railway track runs along the west bank of the Meuse. The military significance of this *defilé* or *cul-de-sac* 'linking' the Argonne ridge and the Heights of the Meuse will be clearly apparent. The Heights of Romagne and Cunel with Barricourt at the head of the reversed triangle comprised the core of the German defensive system between the western edge of the ridge and the Heights of the Meuse. Four main defence lines – five miles apart – lay back in depth from Montfaucon Wood to the Heights of Barricourt. The third position (Kriemhilde), which traversed Romagne and Cunel, was the link in the Hindenburg Line between Alberich and Brunhilde along the line of the Aisne and the Michel Position, which curled north-eastwards to the Moselle. The first position with Montfaucon Wood in the centre ended five miles north of Verdun. The second position (Giselhur) crossed from the Aisne through Montfaucon town almost to the Thinte just east of the Meuse. The fourth position (Freya), which was incomplete, ran from the Bourgogne Wood across the Heights of Barricourt and fell short west of the Meuse.

**Americans assigned to the French XVII Corps advance through Verdun in October**

Hindenburg's Argonne bastion occupied in fact some 420 square miles from the northern part of the forest ridge to the Heights of the Meuse north of Verdun.

General von Gallwitz's assessment of the situation was entirely his own: no word was received from the Supreme Command. And indeed with Prince Max of Baden's campaign to remove the *sergent de bataille* (Erich Ludendorff), Max von Gallwitz was next in line for the Field Marshal's baton. After the St Mihiel battle the general who had jointly commanded *Heeresgruppe Gallwitz* and the German Fifth Army at Verdun detached the latter under the command (on 24th September) of General of Cavalry von der Marwitz. (The appointment of Marwitz came two days after his dismissal from command of the Seventeenth Army for failing to counterattack the British Third Army at Havrincourt on the outlying defences of the Siegfried Position.) The situation at Verdun was no worse than unsettled, but the Fifth Army was weakened by the help given to Fuch's Army Unit C at St Mihiel. Moreover, most of the German divisions numbered nine infantry battalions as opposed to twelve in American divisions.

From Vauquois in the Argonne, a few miles south of Montfaucon Wood, the 7th and 117th Divisions of Reserves (Oven) were stationed as far as the river bank. East of the Meuse Baron von Soden's 1st Austrian Infantry was adjacent to the 15th Infantry Division. On their left ranging to the Michel Position were three more German divisions under Austrian General Goinginger. East of the Meuse the 37th Division lay to the rear. Most of the German soldiers had seen recent action on British and French sectors, and were ostensibly being rested in Lorraine. Two other divisions were near at hand: the 5th Bavarian Reserves were nevertheless below strength and Gallwitz considered another Austrian division devoid of fighting potential. That was the position on the German side ten days before the Battle of the Argonne – most of von der Marwitz's forces were on the other side of the Meuse.

The American First Army was given the tough task of breaking down a traditional symbol of impregnability. Quite apart from the later Hindenburg constructions, camouflaged gun positions and machine-gun posts had been sited and concealed to best advantage amongst the pine trees of the forest since 1915. The formal Foch directive of 6th September ordered that an offensive be undertaken in the direction of Mézières between the Suippe and the Meuse, in which the French Fourth Army (Gouraud) would act jointly with the American First Army under French staff direction. The task for General Gouraud, the one-armed veteran of Gallipoli, was to advance west of the Argonne over less difficult but rocky, hilly terrain towards the plateaux east of the route Rethel – Signy – L'Abbaye. The American Argonne – Meuse operation had for its objective the capture of the Hindenburg Position along the fifteen-mile route Montfaucon – Romagne – Grandpré with a view to overrunning the enemy line Vouziers – Rethel three miles north of the Argonne forest. The French Fourth and American First Armies would rendezvous at the village of Grandpré in the Bourgogne Wood. On the right an American demonstration would be made east of the Meuse. From the Suippe river to the Meuse east of Verdun thirty-seven divisions were summoned to the attack. Along this line on 25th September the German and Austrian armies numbered twenty-four divisions in line and twelve in reserve; but, beginning on 3rd October, the arrival of twenty-seven German divisions strengthened their hand at the

**Camouflaged two-man tanks at Varennes**

expense of their failure to hold the Siegfried and Brunhilde positions further north. The delivery of a *coup de main* in the Argonne depended on Pershing seizing such chances of surprise as existed in the prevailing circumstances. After St Mihiel his staff had less than fourteen days in which to finalise their plans and route half-a-million men, together with equipment and supplies, to the main battle area. In the chill night air peremptory demands to extinguish lights accompanied the progress of the horse-drawn vehicles, motor buses, trucks and battalions of infantry on foot winding their way along the southern roads to the suburbs of Verdun.

The mood of the coming offensive bore comparison with British hopes on the Somme in July 1916. Again a new, vigorous, able-bodied army braced confidently for the first tremors of battle. Doughboys blooded in action on the Marne and St Mihiel mixed with others alighting at improvised railheads from the training areas and replacements straight from the ships. Five conscript divisions were in the forefront of the attack. The French movement control officers at Verdun were well used to the sight of endless files of *poilus* approaching on

**A French gun crew at rest**

the road from Bar-le-Duc; but this time the traffic turned westwards without entering the fortress city. The web of traffic involved four main streams: American occupation of the Argonne sector required the withdrawal of eleven French and Italian divisions; the French II Colonial and XVII Corps were moving up to Pershing's zone of command east of the Meuse, and other French formations were crossing from east to west to reinforce Gouraud's Fourth Army. Artillery tractors crawled along three abreast at ten miles per hour, and traffic chaos was incurred when guns slewed over in the mud. In the daytime tanks, vehicles and guns were camouflaged in laager in the woods, and troops slept in hay lofts, barns and village houses. On 25th September German observation planes counted 382 aircraft belonging to American squadrons on airfields. Surprisingly, until the guns opened fire in the Argonne the following morning and the Germans sent out raiding parties to grab prisoners, they were unaware that American troops were actually west of the Meuse. As the US battalions approached the line of advance, the last retiring French officers threw their bedding rolls on to the backs of trucks, and with expressions of good faith bade their American friends 'good morning'.

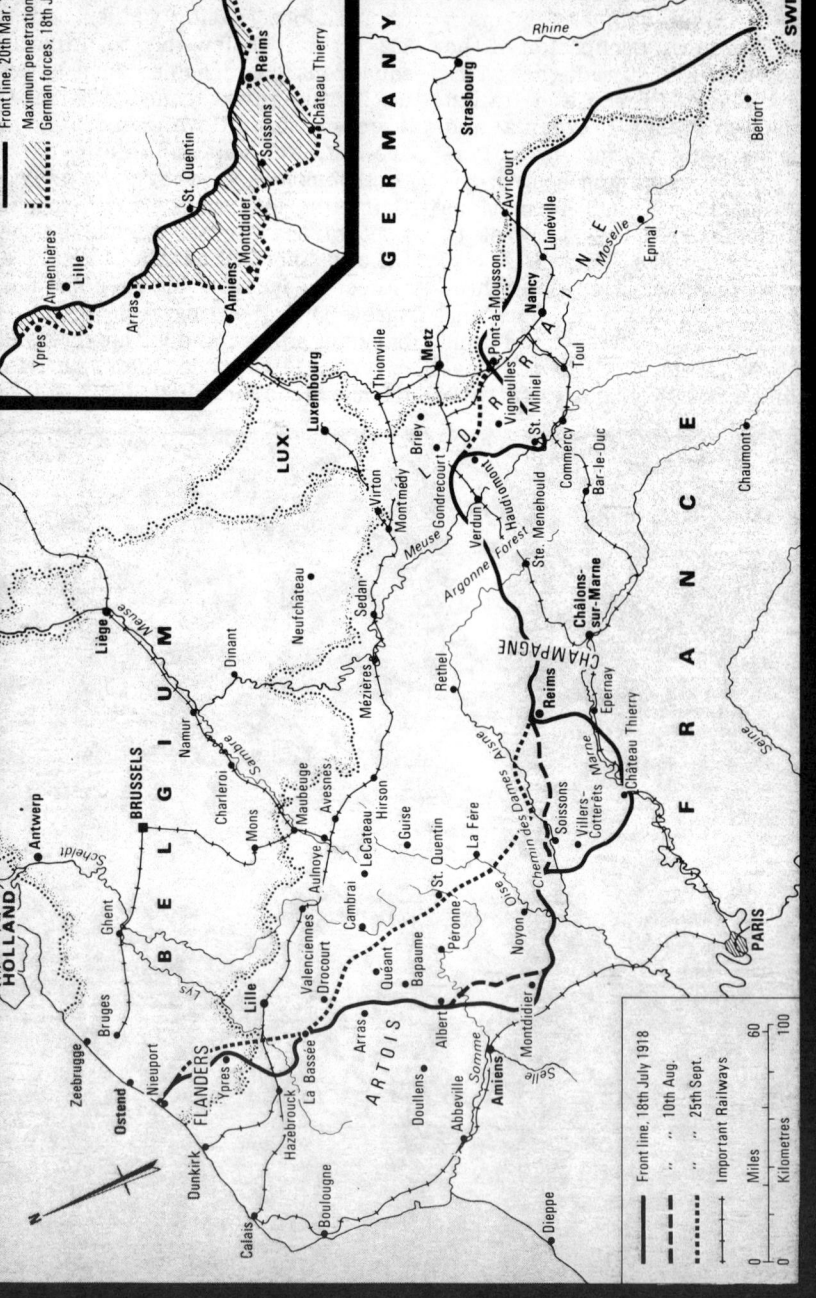

The Western Front in 1918; the Lille-Metz rail line was the objective of the September offensive

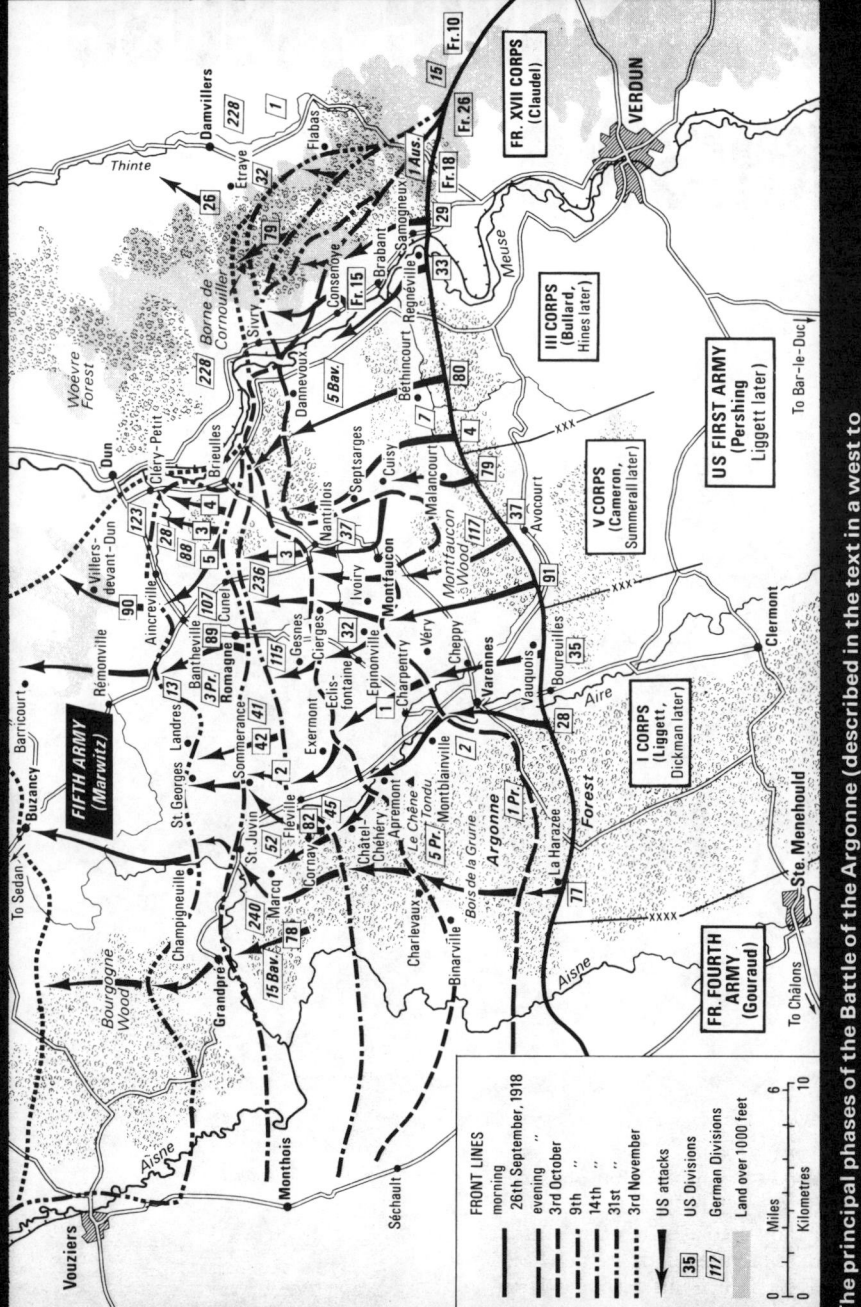

The principal phases of the Battle of the Argonne (described in the text in a west to east sequence). Note that a US division of 28,000 men contained three times the

# The Argonne-Meuse offensive

Command of the Argonne sector passed from Hirschauer's French Second Army to General Pershing on 22nd September. The larger part of the field guns including corps and army artillery material and supplies, were sent up by the French army. Some American divisions were joined by their artillery brigades for the first time, and those divisions without artillery brigades were brought up to strength with French gunners. There was no time to obtain heavy tanks, and about twenty-five per cent of the 189 French light tanks were manned by French crews. 821 Allied aircraft, of which 600 were piloted by American flyers, were concentrated in the St Mihiel area. The scene north of the St Menehould – Verdun road presented a confused panorama of hastily prepared ammunition dumps, gun positions, signal wire and artillery pulled along by emaciated and exhausted teams of horses. Guns were sited and camouflaged in open fields and on the edges of woods; and at the three corps headquarters French staff officers worked alongside the Americans studying air photographs until the last minute to allocate targets to the guns. Inevitably, the French left their legacy of old trenches, craters and roadways dissolved under shell-fire into canyons of mud. Engineers and signallers made their last preparations for the advance: field dressing stations, medical supplies and ambulances were ready to move forward. On the night of 25th

**Rest period for infantry mopping up on the edge of a shattered wood**

**A French Schneider tank returns from the front**

September trench mortar batteries were placed in position and the infantry and machine-gunners moved into the French trenches in anticipation of the dawn attack.

The necessity of securing supplies prevented a long artillery preparation. During the three hours before daybreak the fire of 2,700 guns was brought to bear on the German barbed-wire entanglements, trenches and rear supply areas: predicted fire broke out into a heavy rolling barrage; the French gunners reloading with indifference to the thunderous backlash as shells were flighted across No-Man's Land to their targets. As testimony to the intensity of the barrage, General von Gallwitz recorded that the windows of his headquarters at Montmédy reverberated – at a distance of twenty-five miles – under the noise of the 'new' American general's nocturnal bombardment. German reaction to the barrage, if swift, was restrained by lack of resources to pre-empt a full-scale attack. In the forest between La Harazée and Vauquois the 1st Prussian Guard Division was now assembled on the extreme left flank of the German Third Army. Behind them on the Kriemhilde defence line stood the 5th Prussian Guard in the vicinity of Binarville and Montblainville. The 5th Bavarian Reserves, ordered across from the east bank of the Meuse to cover the rear of Oven's 117th and 7th Reserve Divisions ran into the barrage of Pershing's guns as they continued firing during the day. Raiding parties from the 117th east of Montfaucon Wood crawled out during the night and took prisoners from the 4th Division trenches several hours before the signal to attack was given. As dawn broke the observation balloons went up; aircraft hovered overhead looking for combat opponents and flew out low over the German trenches to observe troop movements. The morning was foggy and grey clouds threatened rain.

At 0530 hours the American infantry climbed out of their trenches along the entire line from La Harazée to Brabant and walked forward in silence at a regular pace. The outlines of the sombre helmeted figures with packs and gasmasks were relieved only by occasional grey flashes of bayonet steel from the points of their extended rifles. In the absence of tanks in the first assault wave engineers urgently tackled barbed wire with Bangalore torpedoes and explosives; gaps created by the 75mm's and trench mortars were open invitations for dangerous enfilade fire from either flank; but damp fuses were painfully slow to burn.

Advancing in unison with the rolling barrage, every man, every platoon was moving on a time schedule. The silent momentum of the advancing battalions was interrupted only when machine-gun fire broke through their ranks and uneven ground disturbed the set pace of the march. When the infantry reached the wire men were everywhere snipping strands and bending them back as they crawled forward within yards of their own shells bursting in the German trenches. Few of the officers and men had ever stormed a first-class fortified line before. They knew the character of the maze of fortifications only from lectures, photographs and maps. They knew with certainty, however, that their job was to kill Germans or take them prisoner. At 0930 hours the assault troops were through the wire and trench systems and out into open country; and the fog – which had been their friend – was dissipated two hours later by bright sunlight radiating warmth in the cold morning air.

Communication with Gouraud's Fourth Army, which attacked at 0600 hours, was maintained on the 77th Divisions' left through the 368th

**The 'Blue Ridge' Division in the Brieulles Wood**

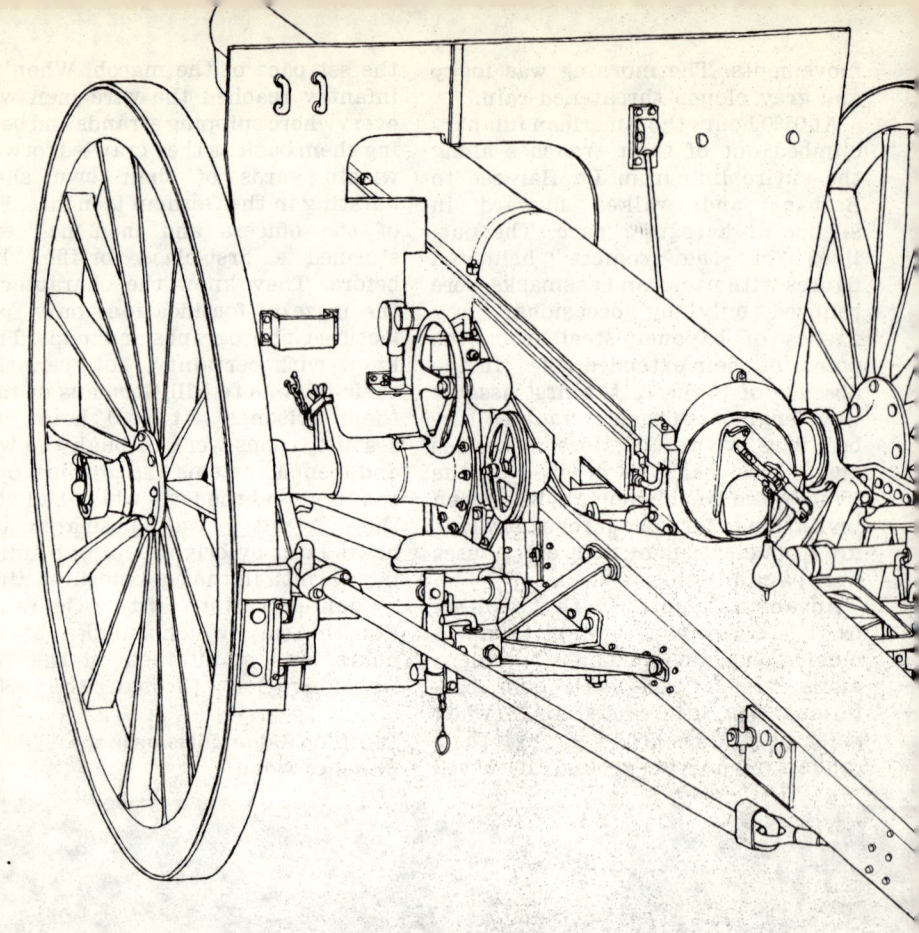

The French 75mm gun. This, one of the world's most celebrated guns ever, was France's artillery mainstay in the First World War. Accurate and with a very high rate of fire, it was an excellent light artillery piece for direct fire. One unfortunate consequence of its capabilities was that the French tended to accept that any light and medium artillery task could be undertaken by the '75', and so development of other weapons was undertaken only slowly. *Calibre:* 75mm. *Weight of shell:* 16lbs. *Maximum range:* 7,440 yards. *Elevation:* –10 to +19 degrees. *Weight:* 2,657lbs. *Rate of fire:* 6 rounds per minute, though 20 rounds a minute could be achieved over short periods by experienced crews

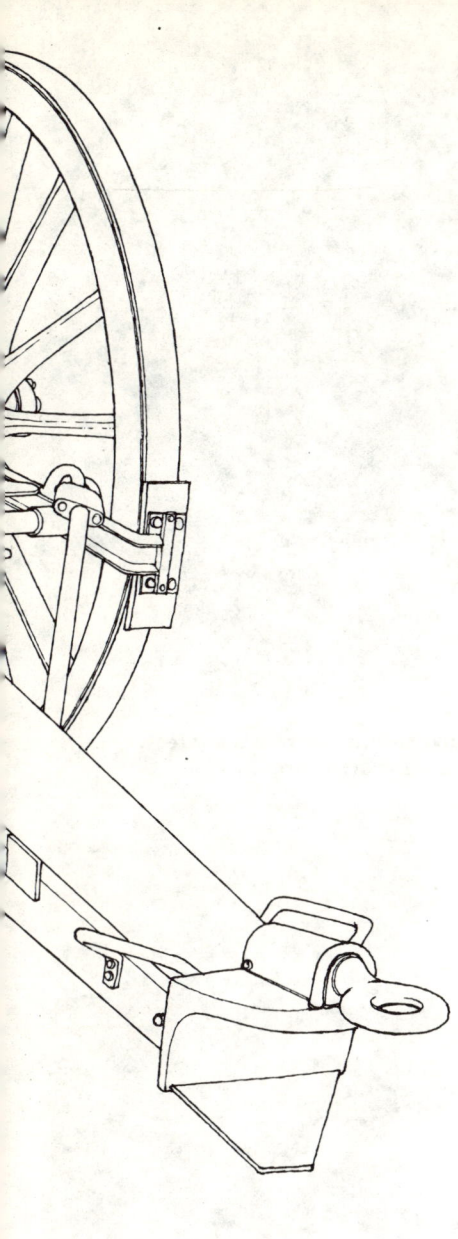

Infantry of the 92nd as part of a Franco-American liaison detachment of the *Groupement Durand*. Alexander's brigades on the forest heights saw little in the early morning fog. Once across the wire, shafts of sunlight lit the way in the forest; but keeping any kind of formation through the dense undergrowth was impractical. The way was littered with the manmade debris of war and tree trunks and branches fallen in the aftermath of storms. Company commanders found liaison with junior officers almost impossible, and even platoon commanders were hard pressed to keep in touch with their men. The rifle platoons were driven from forest paths by ambush fire and, when hit in the middle of the platoon, groups of two or three men went ahead in isolation. As the Prussian Guard became wise to the situation, clusters of machine-gun nests opened deadly fire from crests. Machine-gunners traversed their barrels from side to side across ravines and gullies, and snipers picked off men cutting their paths through yet more strands of wire. When strongpoints were located the infantry brought up 37mm cannon and mortars; they hurled grenades at concealed machine-gun posts and brought out unwilling prisoners at bayonet point. As the day progressed, captured machine-guns accumulated in piles beside forest paths. At dusk the 77th, which had covered 2,500 yards, prepared to continue its advance towards Les Quatres Chênes, on a line with Binarville village lying westwards in the Aisne valley.

The Keystones were astride the Aire, a meandering river with steep escarpments. On the left prominent spurs extended from the ridge on the eastern slopes of the Argonne. On the right was the village of Varennes where, endeavouring to escape from the Revolution in 1791, Louis XVI and Marie Antoinette were captured and returned ignominiously to the Tuileries in Paris. In their first stride, Darrah's 55th Brigade took Perrières Hill and

*Above:* German infantry wait for the doughboys to emerge from the forest.
*Below:* Watching fall of shot from a hillside position in the Argonne

*Above:* 155mm howitzer battery sited in the ruins of Varennes. *Below:* A trench position in the Verdun sector

German prisoners and American wounded on 5th October

the ruins of Varennes, from which point they were in plain view of the Romagne heights. The Germans had substituted light railways for the shell-torn roads, but tanks made some headway in this neighbourhood against *Landwehr* machine-gunners. In a leading tank a corporal, almost choked with gas by the explosion of a shell, threw himself into a shell-hole for safety, but ran back thirty yards under heavy machine-gun fire to rescue his officer who was trapped in the blazing machine. The 56th Brigade (Colonel Rickards) advanced along the southern slope of the Argonne, but was unable to overcome intense machine-gun fire from the Prussian Guard on Champ Mahaut, a prominent spur overlooking Varennes. During the day the right-hand brigade advanced three miles on to high ground south of La Forge, and from this position they could see le Chêne Tondu, a wooded promontory that stuck out of the Argonne and commanded the breadth of the Meuse valley. Beyond this lay the even stronger heights called Taille l'Abbé. The 28th Division was unable to make further progress that day as the men could not get the support they needed from either flank.

McClure's 69th Infantry Brigade led 35th Division's attack and quickly went astride Vauquois hill and Rossignol Wood, leaving supporting troops to clean up and take Vauquois itself. The 117th Reserves, occupying a limited area around and to the west of Malancourt, at first held their ground, but the retreat of the 7th Reserves on their left soon made its impact felt. Clearing a path east of Varennes, left-hand battalions shared in the capture of the town with the 28th Division. Conveyed in motor trucks across the Meuse valley, the 5th Bavarian Reserves put up disjointed but spirited resistance forward of the Giselhur Position. Advance companies of the 69th Infantry Brigade ran into the barbed wire and concrete pillboxes at Cheppy. When the 138th Infantry was held back by machine-gun fire, Captain Alexander Skinker waved his company down and ran forward with an automatic rifleman and carrier to direct fire on the pillboxes from a gap in the wire. The carrier was killed instantly, but Captain Skinker continued to feed ammunition to the rifleman until he himself was killed. Another company of the 138th was similarly restricted at Cheppy until Private Wold advanced with another man and silenced a group of pillboxes. Jumping into a trench he shot a German officer who was about to kill a comrade, and was himself killed in his attempt to rush a fifth machine-gun post. The advance of Company I was entirely due to his resourcefulness. Cheppy was captured and as night approached the leading brigade was well down the Aire about three miles from the start-line. After taking high ground south of Charpentry, Liggett pulled back Traub's division to a line from the Aire to a point a few hundred yards north of Véry.

West of Montfaucon Wood Johnston's 91st Division with his two in-

The advance to Montfaucon in V Corps sector

fantry brigades in line abreast swept through Cheppy Wood in rapid movement four miles to the Giselhur defence works at Epinonville. Machine-gun battalions, undeterred by the first line trench systems, dragged their guns forward on carts, and infantry chafing for artillery support were rewarded when the 75mms were unhooked and manoeuvred into position to pound German machine gun emplacements. After having his attention deflected by the St Mihiel operation, Gallwitz was now actively reinforcing Oven's troops in the centre around Montfaucon. During the afternoon the 5th Bavarian Reserves, which had been hit hard by the opening bombardment, were ordered to advance; at 1700 hours two regiments of the 37th Infantry Division strongly counterattacked at Ivoiry. Any attempts to strengthen these counter-movements were thwarted nevertheless by chaos on the shell-cratered roadways and narrow gauge tracks leading south from Romagne and Cunel. Again passage by company to the Giselhur Line was made possible by the heroism of individual soldiers. In the morning fog Sergeant West of D Company, 363rd Infantry, directed fire of an automatic rifle section eliminating two machine-gun posts in Cheppy Wood. Sergeant Seibert of F Company, 364th Infantry, charged a machine-gun post in advance of his company at Epinonville, and carried back wounded soldiers until he collapsed with exhaustion. In the evening the leading brigade was driven from Epinonville; and Eclisfontaine on the Romagne road was evacuated as an artillery barrage was to be laid through the town during the night.

Farnsworth's National Guardsmen from Ohio and West Virginia in the centre of V Corps' front had the most important objective of the day. But the 37th had an advantage over the divisions on either flank - a shade more experience. The hill town of Montefaucon in the centre of Giselhur was the highest point on the way to the Lille – Metz railway line, with the exception of the Buzancy heights on the northern extremity of the Argonne – Meuse sector. The railway track was in fact visible from the old German first-line trench system at Malancourt. Moving forward from Avocourt on the Châlons – Verdun road towards Cierges and Rémonville, Zimerman's 73rd and Jackson's 74th Infantry Brigades pushed through Monfaucon Wood encountering stiff resistance on the left of the line. In the open country that lay between the wood and Montfaucon hill, the 117th Reserves did not linger in retreat to form defence lines. When the division headed into the open country both brigades were caught in crossfire from numerous small hills. Battalions broke up into marauder packs of hunters to engage sources of fire aimed from every direction. One company which remained grouped together was destroyed almost to a man when, after sighting a quarry and seizing the high ground forming the south-western approach from the wood to Montfaucon town, they unthinkingly exposed themselves in silhouette on the treeless skyline. Fortunately for Farnsworth, the left flank of the afternoon counterattack was weakened when two Bavarian regiments were bogged down in the traffic chaos in Romagne. Cameron at Corps headquarters had little reliable news from the division during the day; but Montfaucon had not fallen, and at the end of the day Farnsworth's division was grouped at random along a line from a point 800 yards south of Ivoiry in the west to the foot of Montfaucon hill.

On the right of the Corps area Kuhn's division advanced from the Avocourt sector east of Montfaucon Wood uphill in the direction of Montfaucon town and Cunel Wood. What was left of the ruins of Haucourt and Malancourt was built into the trench system they had to cross. Nicholson's 157th Brigade captured Haucourt on the left and Noble's 158th Brigade overran Malancourt on the right.

Spreading out in open country the division met with the same kind of resistance encountered by the 37th Division. Units of Nicholson's brigade shared the capture of Cuisy Wood with Jackson's 74th Infantry Brigade after a three-hour struggle on the left. Although the centre units progressed to Hill 294 and beyond to the southern slopes of Montfaucon hill, they were rebuffed by continuous artillery and machine-gun fire and were obliged to fall back into line with the left and right flanks. In the afternoon French tanks across the Malancourt road, leading northwards to Cunel, ran into trouble from a German battery firing from the northern edge of Montfaucon Wood and six of the tanks were destroyed. At the close of the day although units had reached Montfaucon hill by the late afternoon the divisional front was stabilised about two miles from the start-line – a mile beyond Malancourt and in line with the northern edge of Cuisy Wood. Other units of the 37th Infantry Division, which threw two regiments forward at Ivoiry at 1700 hours, were around Montfaucon, the entire division backing Oven's 117th Reserves.

Hines' 4th Division on the left of Bullard's Corps area made a spectacular advance of seven miles across the Giselhur line capturing Septsarges; participating with the right of the 79th in the occupation of Cuisy. Unfortunately, due to a misinterpretation of orders, an opportunity to take Montfaucon was lost during the afternoon. With the 7th Brigade (Poore) leading the way, both infantry brigades moved off on the Malancourt road; but after two miles trudging along the shell-torn trail of craters they turned north-eastwards into open country in their own sector. After repulsing, without artillery support, three counterattacks in the afternoon east of Montfaucon by the German 7th and units of the 5th Bavarian Reserves, the two brigades with the 8th (Booth) on the right went astride of Nantillois and on to high ground through Brieulles Wood. Leading companies on the left of the 7th Brigade tried unsuccessfully for Fays Wood on the south-eastern limits of the Cunel heights, and which was within machine-gun range from the Kriemhilde Line. Although the Brieulles Wood was not entirely clear of defenders, the division was firmly established by nightfall in the belt of forest which connects the Cunel heights through Fays and Brieulles Woods across high ground to the west bank of the Meuse. The regular division had left the open country of the Meuse valley behind them and was in similar terrain at the head of the defile to the 77th Division ten miles westwards on the Argonne ridge. On the right the Blue Ridge Division was heading for the same timber country.

The 80th (Blue Ridge) Division attacked with the 160th Infantry Brigade (Brett) leading on the right south of Béthincourt, and crossed Forges brook before clearing part of a wood of the same name. On the left after an all-day fight, Jameson's 159th Infantry Brigade forced its way past strong positions on Hill 262 and reached the reverse slopes of the hill a few miles east of Septsarges. The right-hand brigade went through Juré Wood and established its line north of Dannevoux, which meant a march of just over four miles from the start-line. The small town of Dannevoux lies near the southern edge of the Brieulles slope a mile or so from the Meuse river bank. Every move Cronkhite's division made in the valley could be seen from Montfaucon hill in the west and in the east from the menacing Borne de Cornouiller (or Hill 378) on the opposite bank of the Meuse. Observers on Hill 378 could look down on everything from the Verdun forts to the Kriemhilde line. The division, not as far forward as the 4th, was subjected to continual artillery and machine-gun fire from Brieulles Wood, and it was to take three days of stiff fighting to get on to the high ground. After the first day the

*Above:* Lieutenant Latham, a dentist by profession, works under difficult conditions in a dugout in the Meuse valley. *Below:* Captured German 105mm gun. *Right:* Americans use camouflage left by the Germans in Forges Wood.

divisional front extended from the northern edge of Septsarges Wood almost to the Meuse east of Dannevoux.

Bell's 33rd Division from Illinois advanced under covering fire from a hill called Mort Homme, and wheeled right through the Forges Wood to occupy the west bank of the Meuse. The 66th Infantry Brigade (Wolf) attacking from Bois Trench north of Regnéville captured the larger part of Forges Wood and the village and also helped the Blue Ridge Division on their left to clear the Juré Wood. Passage along the river bank was made difficult by swamps and creeks; and engineers building bridges and footbridges with fascines and planks were always under intense fire from the Heights of the Meuse. The engineers, who were actively engaged in making divisional roadways along the entire front, were sitting targets for machine-gunners in low-flying aircraft. The division captured a German engineer depot, thirty guns, dozens of machine-guns, a light railway and took six enemy prisoners to every Illinois man lost. The 132nd Infantry got three Medals of Honor in Forges Wood. Sergeant Gumpertz, E Company, started with two others for a machine-gun post when his companions were killed by a shellburst. The sergeant went on alone, jumped into the nest and brought out nine prisoners. Sergeant Sandlin, A Company, killed the crew of another machine-gun post with a grenade enabling the company to advance. Captain Mallon was separated in the early morning fog from his company together with nine men. Throughout the day they acted independently attacking hostile machine-gunners and in the afternoon rushed a four piece 155mm howitzer battery, which they took intact with the crew. Captain Mallon's group in addition to the howitzer battery cap-

*German prisoners carry their wounded to an American field dressing station*

tured eleven machine-guns, an anti-aircraft gun and one hundred prisoners.

The 33rd Division was both hinge and flank protection for Pershing's left arm sweeping across the Argonne to the Hindenburg Line. But Bell's National Guardsmen fulfilled the equally important function of pivot to the American First Army on the left and the Franco-American force on the right between the Meuse and the Moselle. East of the Meuse French XVII Corps was adjacent to French II (Colonial) Corps, which included the 26th Yankee Division, and Dickman's IV Corps was on the far right. Counting II Corps (the 27th and 30th Divisions) on the Somme twenty-three American divisions were committed to the line at the end of September. The progress on the Argonne sector on the first day of the offensive was good; and moreover in the case of the 4th Division's advance to Brieulles Wood, of an exceptional nature. General Pétain was of the belief that the American First Army would do well to take Montfaucon before midwinter. General Pershing expected however that the vigour and aggression of his troops would make up for their lack of experience and technical skills. The opening advance was made by nine divisions, which succeeded in breaking down the first line defences against stubborn resistance from three enemy divisions. During the day the German front line troops were joined by elements of two other divisions. The second line of defences (Giselhur) was overrun in places but Montfaucon in the centre was firmly in German hands. Pershing had every reason to proceed with caution. Gallwitz had already ordered considerable reinforcement of the German army in the Argonne. Half Pershing's tank force had been destroyed. The American First Army was boxed on three sides by the Kriemhilde Line and flank fire from the Argonne Ridge and the Heights of the Meuse. The question of supply gave much cause for concern. The whole terrain in front of the first line position was one continuous area of deep shell holes; and the roads leading north were all but impassable to artillery and supply trains.

The Battle of the Argonne could not be delayed. Time taken for readjustments would invite counterattacks and the proper repair of the roads would take many weeks. The Foch timetable for the victory offensive had gone according to plan. On the Saturday King Albert's army was on the move between Armentières and the sea and on the Sunday Rawlinson's British Fourth and Debeney's French First Armies made the frontal assault on the Siegfried Position. Even at this late stage the irrepressible Marshal Foch sent General Weygand to the American sector with the offer of the French Second Army to ensure that Pershing effected the right-hand pincer movement in the Argonne. The bright sun that broke through on the first day was seen no more: when Clemenceau visited the captured ruins of Montfaucon under heavy shellfire on Sunday 29th September the morning was raw and damp; and the weather got colder and wetter as the weeks passed by.

The German Supreme Command quickly transferred Group Argonne (von Kleist) from the left wing of the Third Army to the control of *Heersgruppe Gullwitz*. Army Unit C on the Woëvre was also attached to this sphere of command. On 29th September the Group Kleist sector covered eight miles of the Argonne from Binarville in the Aisne valley across the ridge in the vicinity of Le Chêne Tondu to beyond Apremont on the Aire. The 1st Guard Division, rated as one of the Kaiser's best shock forma-

*A 14-inch gun shells a troop concentration area in the rear of the Kriemhilde Line*

tions, did not resist as strongly as it might have done; but after four years of constant fighting the morale of the Prussians was low. The comparatively new 5th Guard Division, recently in the Second Battle of the Marne, was also known to be a first-class division. Both the 1st and 5th Guards were withdrawn after heavy losses on 8th October; the 3rd Grenadiers of the latter being completely annihilated.

The 2nd *Landwehr* Division in the forest and across the Aire valley fought hard and well throughout the Battle of the Argonne. These elderly Swabians from the Kingdom of Württemberg put most of Patton's tanks out of action on the Varennes sector with sticks and hand grenades. The first-class 52nd Division, transferred from Bapaume, reinforced the front near Exermont on the southern edge of the Romagne heights. The 45th Reserves, which had an average reputation, was in the forest west of Châtel-Chéhéry. This division was weakened in morale by replacement troops with strong Bolshevik sympathies. Some of the men were shot for refusing orders, and others deserted to the American lines. None of the German divisions were entirely at full strength, and at one stage of the battle the 2nd *Landwehr* held com-

*Above:* German casualties in a sunken road on the Wotan position (Drocourt-Quéant Switch). *Below:* American casualties are moved to the rear.
*Right:* Deep in the forest, men of 77th Division who were recruited largely from the tenements and lodging houses of New York

panies in the line with only twenty-five men.

Between 27th September and 1st October the 77th Division launched a series of attacks through the Bois de la Grurie and made a line 800 yards east of Binarville through the Bois de la Naza to the south-western approach to Le Chêne Tondu. With seemingly nothing but forest ahead and vision soon reduced to a few yards, Alexander's 'Liberty' men would have been excused for thinking they were fighting the war on their own. Communication with XXXVIII Corps of Fourth Army on the Aisne and with the Keystones across the escarpments of the Aire was a nightmare. Seeking flanking manoeuvres, American regimental commanders quickly lost touch with their battalions, and it was left to company and platoon commanders to fight their way as best they could across the deep undergrowth. Fire support depended on the machine-gunners and 37mm cannon; angles of sight on field guns being barred by the tops of the pine trees. Enemy artillery sited on the edges of the ridge were on occasion though turned inwards on the invaders with devastating effect.

Capturing a treacherous ravine south-east of Binarville on the 29th the advance made a big swing on the right of the ridge. When contact was lost between a battalion of the 308th Infantry Regiment and the regimental command post, Lieutenant-Colonel Fred Smith went forward with two other officers and ten soldiers to re-establish runner posts and carry ammunition to the front line. When the party strayed out of reach of supporting fire, they came under machine-gun fire at fifty yards. Shouting to his party to take cover, Smith drew his pistol and killed the German gun crew. Although badly wounded, he made his way back to collect hand grenades, and was later killed locating another machine-gun emplacement.

Contact was lost with another battalion of the 308th when Captain

McMurty's company was completely surrounded near Charlevaux. Captain McMurty, who was hit by shrapnel in the knee, organised bearers to carry the wounded to shelter. On the second day food ran out, and there was little water to drink. The company continued to resist under machine-gun and rifle fire that seldom let up for seven days. When the position was relieved, McMurty – by now suffering also from a grenade wound in the shoulder – led out the survivors and refused hospital attention until proper care had been taken of the wounded. When K Company of the same regiment was held back by fire from a single machine-gun emplacement, Sergeant Kaufman took out a patrol to silence the gun. Separated from the other men, his right arm shattered, Kaufman crawled into a favourable position and threw grenades with his left hand. Finally when he charged the emplacement with an empty pistol he took one prisoner and scattered the rest of the crew.

On 1st October Johnson's 154th Brigade charged down the tree-covered slopes of the Charlevaux ravine, across streams and swamps and up the slopes on the other side. On the next day an even deeper advance was made across the Fontaine-aux-Charmes ravine and on to the Heights of Le Chêne Tondu. The 77th Division had covered six miles in six days. When the leading brigade attacked on 2nd October, the 308th Infantry was again in trouble. Major Charles Whittlesey with six companies from the 1st Battalion, assisted by elements of the 307th Infantry and 306th Machine Gun Battalion, penetrated an enemy fire line north-east of Binarville between the Bois de la Buisonne and the Moulin de Charlevaux. The group found itself encircled in a ravine east of the Charlevaux Mill. Contact was maintained with the men on that day and a company of the 307th got through to them. The Germans however wedged troops between the stranded companies and the main body of the division. They were a mile ahead of the front line and were exposed to machine-gun fire from all sides of the ravine. Major Whittlesey held his command and defended the Binarville ravine for five days. Two-day rations were soon exhausted and the men confessed to eating leaves to alleviate their hunger. The only water available was in a swamp stream constantly under fire in the centre of the ravine. The besieged men salvaged rifles and ammunition from the dead men lying beside them. The Air Service flew in food, medical supplies and ammunition, but none of these supplies reached the men in the ravine. Survivors later said they were sickened by a phosphorescent glow that rose from blood on the corpses of German and American soldiers. When Prussian officers sent Whittlesey a written proposition to surrender, the battalion commander refused the terms with contempt. Major Whittlesey's 'Lost Battalion' came out on 7th October with less than half of the 463 officers and men who were originally trapped in the Binarville ravine. On 8th October Alexander's division was concentrated on a front a mile south of Châtel-Chéréry and within three miles of the Romagne heights across the Fléville gap.

On 27th September Muir's divisional front was dominated by the Heights of Champ Mahaut, but the 28th Division captured Montblainville lying to the north-east on the Aire late that day. On the next day the 55th and 56th Brigades (now Nolan and Conger) astride the road to Romagne approached Apremont on the route to Fléville. Nolan's Brigade on the left scaled the steep cliffs of Le Chêne Tondu under heavy fire. This daring assault gave I Corps possession of part of the heights before the 77th went through, eliminating a vitally important source of flank fire across the valley. Apremont fell on the 28th, and the right-hand brigade swung out to the east through the open country.

But without adequate support from the divisional guns and in the face of determined counterattacks by the *Landwehr*, Muir's division took eight days to reach the Fléville gap. The advance was controlled to an extent, of course, by the progress of the 77th on the ridge. The Argonne forest was all but cleared of the German army by the morning of 8th October; but I Corps' job was to seize the southwestern corner of the Romagne heights as well. Apart from the northernmost tip near Grandpré, the spurs associated with the Fléville gap and almost linking the ridge with the Romagne heights were the only areas of the forest terrain still to be taken. And it was here – defending the gap at Châtel-Chéréry and Cornay – that what was left of two Prussian divisions and the mutinous 45th Reserves was concentrated. Although the depleted Prussian divisions were later pulled out, General von Gallwitz was prepared to fight hard on 8th October to deny I Corps a foothold in the Kriemhilde Line.

On the night 6th/7th October Lindsey's 164th Infantry Brigade of the 82nd Division marched eight miles and took station along the road to La Forge 400 yards south of Fléville. The following day the Keystone Division captured the town of Châtel-Chéréry and on the far right occupied several hills north-east of Apremont. As the conscript brigade, which had been in reserve since before St Mihiel, was lined up on the road the troops could see the battle for Hill 223 north of Châtel-Chéréry. The brigade was split up: three battalions captured Hills 180 and 240 with great energy and dash; the other half of the brigade preparing to relieve the Keystones on Hill 223 during the night, as a springboard for the brigade morning attack. In the morning the corps was destined to make a successful assault on the last German strongpoints on the Argonne Ridge. The 2nd Battalion of the 328th Infantry Regiment crossed the Aire over a shaky footbridge and marched at a brisk pace through Châtel-Chéréry under shell-fire and started to dig in on Hill 223. Their objective was the narrow gauge Décauville rail track bringing the last supplies into the forest area from Grandpré. In the morning the three battalions advanced from Hill 223 without artillery support into a succession of valleys. The 2nd Battalion entered a triangular shaped valley with steep sides covered in thicket and rock-strewn bushes. Almost from the beginning the battalion was split in half by German machine-gun fire sweeping into the valley from both sides. In the confusion G Company was broken up, and Captain Danforth lost contact with his platoons in the rear.

The heaviest fire was coming from concealed positions on the left, and Sergeant Parsons ordered half his platoon to work their way round the valley through dense bushes to locate the machine-gun emplacements from the rear. Three squads dropped back and were ready to move in file to the left of the company's line of advance. Meeting only a few stray bullets on the way, the party of seventeen men skirted the left side of the valley and found themselves near the first line machine-gun defences. Some of the men were in favour of a flank attack, but Sergeant Early and Corporal Alvin York decided to press on further, swing in suddenly and jump the machine-gunners from the rear. But some Germans with Red Cross bands appeared without warning and one was shot as they started to run to give the alarm. Jumping a stream, the Americans came face-to-face with twenty Germans who threw up their hands in surrender. Sergeant Early then led his party through trees into a clearing to find a German company headquarters. Situated in a second line position, the officers were sitting down to breakfast in the open, unaware that enemy troops were anywhere near. At the same time machine-gunners on the high ground spotted the arrival of the American troops and concentrated

111

Sergeant Alvin Callum York, the last of the long hunters, on the hill near Châtel-Chéréry on which his raid took place

their guns on friend and foe alike in their own position. Early and Cutting were badly wounded and Savage fell dead with over a hundred bullets in his body. Six of the privates were either killed or wounded. Corporal York rallied the seven fit survivors and they were at once ready to fight their way out of a dangerous situation.

Corporal Alvin York, reared in the tradition of the long hunters of Tennessee and Kentucky, was a marksman. When a German officer and five men with bayonets charged, York picked them off with a pistol one by one, starting with the man in the rear. That was the way he shot wild turkeys at home when he did not want the front ones to know what was happening. Twenty Germans had been killed, but the Americans' predicament was still acute. Later York surprised a German officer near a stream. He was about to fire when the German officer volunteered to surrender with fifty prisoners if he had the American's word that he would not kill them. The prisoners were duly assembled, but York was forced to kill the officer when the latter was about to throw a hand grenade at him. When the batch of prisoners had grown to about ninety in number, Corporal York boldly decided to form them up in column and march them right across the German front line trenches to his battalion area in the valley below. At this time machine-gun nests were still firing on either side of his proposed route into the valley. Determined not to leave the wounded behind York instructed the Germans to bring them to the column, so that they could be carried through the lines. He then distributed his seven men along the flanks of the column, and led a battalion commander to the front with a .45 Colt firmly in the major's back. The major, who had lived in Chicago and spoke good English, several times tried to lead the party the wrong way – but the corporal was not fooled. Every time they passed a machine-gun post a prod in the back prompted the officer

A ruined church in Exermont

to blow his whistle and call on the crews to surrender.

The battalion headquarters was located on a hillside at the entrance to the valley west of Hill 223. In the words of the battalion adjutant, First Lieutenant Joseph A Woods: 'I personally saw Corporal York and seven privates returning down the hillside on which our PC was located. They had 132 prisoners with them, including three German officers, one a battalion commander. I personally counted the prisoners when Corporal York reported the detachment of prisoners. Corporal York was in entire charge of this party and was marching at the head of the column with the German officers. The seven men with Corporal York were scattered along the flanks and rear of the column. Sergeant Early and Corporal Cutting were being assisted at the rear of the column.' Corporal York, who was later promoted to sergeant, became the all-time American hero. He won the Congressional Medal of Honor, French Legion of Honour, Croix de Guerre with palms, Médaille Militaire, Italian War Cross and other awards as well. As a conscientious objector Alvin C York was refused exemption from army service on several occasions. His diary reveals loyalties genuinely divided between his church – the Church of Christ in Christian Union – and a sense of patriotism and duty to the state. His willingness to go into the line was based on his awareness of the national idea so clearly expressed within the ranks of his own company and platoon. He was prepared to fight because 'they were all my buddies'.

In Group von Oven in the Meuse valley both the 117th and 7th Reserves were rested by 29th September, having suffered a combined loss of 6,700 casualties. The 7th Division – recruited from Prussian Saxony and Thuringia – was back in action on the Kriemhilde Line in mid-October. The 5th Bavarians, which fought bravely at Montfaucon and Dannevoux in the early stages, were not relieved at all during the offensive. The 37th Infantry Division, which was originally all-Prussian and now augmented by Alsace-Lorrainers picked up on the Russian front, was moved westwards from Montfaucon on 1st October to Exermont below Romagne town. A first-class shock division, its Marshal von Hindenburg Regiment was cited for gallantry during the struggle for Kriemhilde. The 115th and 236th Divisions, both from the Rhineland, were in the fight until mid-October. The 115th was involved in very heavy fighting at Gesnes and in the recapture and second defence of the town. The 41st Reserves from West Prussia, which was on the Roumanian front in 1917 and regarded as of poor standard, was in reserve on 6th October at Sommerance just east of Grandpré. The toll of casualties was so heavy that in the case of the 5th Bavarians, for example, initial company combat strengths of sixty were reduced to twenty. Comparative infantry strengths vastly favoured the Americans: but from the grim fortress strongholds German artillery fire was far more effective than that of the Franco-American gun crews. Also the deployment of tanks by the American First Army was not blessed with any degree of success. Almost the entire force was wiped out in the battle; tank crews suffering as much at the hands of individual grenadiers as from the fire of mobile guns.

On 27th September Traub's 35th Division with the 70th Infantry Brigade (Colonel Walker) in the line was stationed between the southern edge of Montrebeau Wood and L'Espérance. The men from Kansas and Missouri were confronted by a series of foothills and hills still higher commanded the valleys and reverse slopes beyond culminating in wooded hills in front of the Kriemhilde Line. At Fléville the floor of the Aire river valley forms a trough. Beyond Montrebeau Wood is the deep broad Exermont ravine. The village of Exermont, which was Traub's main goal, lies in the middle of the ravine.

The brigade attack was launched at 0500 hours with limited support from only one group of guns. From their strongly reinforced commanding position at Charpentry – a key point in the defence line – the Germans sent down artillery and machine-gun fire at the advancing brigade, which was hit also from both flanks. A tank attack was quickly repelled, and exposed American infantry were forced to find cover in gullies, behind banks and in shell holes. In the late afternoon some

divisional artillery was brought up after a tremendous struggle to transport the guns from the rear. In the first flush of success Walker's brigade captured Charpentry and Baulny, but the 9th Infantry Brigade (Nuttman) was quickly ordered up in support. While forward units pressed through Montrebeau Wood the main line started to dig in near Baulny. The division was short of food, and the casualty rate amongst the officers trying to maintain liaison between units was high. The supply problem was made more acute by perfectly registered fire from German guns on to the southern approaches to Charpentry and Baulny. Some men reached the village in the ravine but none could stay alive. On the 29th strong German counterattacks using mobile guns and infantry cannon with devastating effect enforced the withdrawal of the Americans from Exermont and Montrebeau Wood to a ridge northeast of Baulny.

On 1st October the 1st Division moved up via Cheppy and relieved the National Guardsmen at Baulny. The 35th had advanced six miles for a loss of 6,312 casualties. Half the infantry were dead or wounded, and those that survived had barely slept for five days. Extending their front eastwards, Summerall's regulars retook Montre-

*Above:* Major-General William H Johnston observes the progress of 91st Division. *Left:* Artillery traffic in Fléville

beau Wood; Parker's 1st Brigade was on the left, moving along the eastern wall of the Aire under flank fire from the Argonne ridge. On the right was Bamford's 2nd Brigade, moving swiftly in files down into the Exermont ravine. In the village troops who had earlier bunched together across the paths of enfilade fire lay dead in heaps along the wayside. Crossing the ravine (4th October) the right of Bamford's brigade charged the wooded slopes of the Montrefagne, or Hill 240. Twice that day they took the hill, and were twice driven away. Again the Germans used roving guns attached to the infantry with great success, and they were adept at extricating them under pressure and renewing fire from concealed positions. The left-hand brigade advanced three miles and sent patrols out as far as Fléville. The divisional objective was to drive a human wedge across the hills to Kriemhilde and seize high ground overlooking the Aire trough. When, on 5th October, the wooded slopes of Montrefagne fell, the wedge broadened and was made stronger. Fléville changed hands several times, but three days later the division was strongly established on one side of the Aire trough as far as Fléville. The right-hand brigade extending its line to Hill 269 was in part ahead of V Corps and the 181st Brigade of the 91st Division came under Summerall's wing.

After the evacuation of Epinonville five miles west of Montfaucon, Johnston's 91st Division regained the offensive and with one brigade in line passed through Eclisfontaine and fanned out to the left and right of the road. The battalions on the left went through Cierges Wood and temporarily held Gesnes-en-Argonne. But after gaining a foothold in the Morine and Chêne Sec Woods, the brigade could not hold on without support and was driven back through Gesnes with heavy losses.

On 1st October Haan's 32nd Division took over the sector and after two days pushed forward on a new front on a line from the northern edge of Cierges Wood to la Grange-aux-Bois. As the 91st had learned to its cost, if an element of one division made a gain, it must have the support of gains by the divisions on both flanks. Moving in concert with the 1st on the left and Buck's 3rd Division on the right, Haan's most vital assignment was to remove the danger of crossfire on the 1st Division from the western wall of the Aire and the hills in front of his own division. By 4th October Gesnes was recaptured, but the fall of Cierges merely exposed the division in front of Cunel Wood at the foot of the heights. The field of approach to the Kriemhilde Line was commanded by the strengthened defences on the surrounding hills. McCoy's 63rd Infantry Brigade reached the summit of Hill 239 due east of the village of Gesnes. To the west the Morine and Chêne Sec Woods form a single oblong patch, and the divisional artillery pounded these woods for several days. When on the same day the First Army attacked in unison along the entire front, the 32nd – nicknamed 'The Arrows' – could make little further progress against a welter of machine-gun and artillery fire, and they were raked by bullets from German planes. In a day of ceaseless endeavour the Arrows made no more than 800 yards.

Although Summerall's division had driven its wedge in the right place, it was not as wide as the general wanted it to be. The bluff above Fléville called for hard driving by both the 1st and the 32nd. Setting his heart on the capture of the Morine and Chêne Sec Woods and Hill 255 beyond, Haan concentrated his artillery fire on the area and at night-time the woods and hill were lit up by the fall of high explosive and incendiary shells. At 0630 hours on the 5th three battalions of infantry began an assault on the woods over terrain covered with new shell-craters, smashed machine-gun nests and the litter of fallen trees. The gunners were unable, however, to stifle the machine-gun fire coming from hidden recesses on the forward slope of Hill 255. Meanwhile the left and centre were stopped by encircling fire north of Gesnes. Demands for increased support by the American artillery were met, but it was not enough to break the ring of fire. Counterattacks by the 115th Division in the neighbourhood of Gesnes were numerous. This German division – which since 1916 had been in Russia and Roumania – was badly shaken by the French army on the Marne. With renewed vigour the Rhinelanders drove the 32nd back and retook Gesnes, but the American left-hand brigade held on to a wood west of the village below the Romagne heights. In a change of boundaries the division was given a little extra territory on the right by the 3rd Division, but relinquished the sector south of Gesnes to the northern perimeter of the Chêne Sec Wood to the 181st Infantry Brigade attached to the right of the 91st Division. In summary Haan's division had made little progress at the entrance to the Romagne/Cunel gap and remained exposed in a vulnerable location.

Having cleared Montfaucon Wood on the first day, Farnworth's 37th Division with the 79th on the right challenged Montfaucon town by 1100 hours on 27th September. Crowding every available man into the battle, the 37th was subjected to widespread artillery fire and the long-range sweep of bullets. In the onward movement field guns stalled and gunners used snatch ropes to drag the guns forward in the wet mud, but engineers succeeded in building a road through Montfaucon Wood. In three days of heavy fighting the men fought themselves to a complete standstill. Zimerman's 79th Brigade entered Emont Wood south of Cierges, but the position was made untenable when the Germans pumped in deadly phosgene gas. Capturing Beuge Wood on the right Jackson's 74th Brigade advanced to within 400 yards of the Cierges – Nantillois road. After their eviction from Emont Wood, the left-hand brigade was forced into cover to recuperate from the gas attack. Throwing an infantry ring around the wood, ten light tanks went into action on the western edge of the wood; but after letting the tanks manoeuvre, the Germans destroyed them all with fire from mobile guns. Although a patrol located a water point, the division ran out of food on the third day. At night the men fell dispiritedly on to the wet earth, and lay without blankets in an advanced state of fatigue and sickness from exposure. While the National Guardsmen were entrenching, patrols dodging shellbursts probed the Cierges defences, but without adequate artillery support the men were hardly in a fit state to attack anyway. A call from the 91st Division to help their brigade holding on grimly to Gesnes was delayed but, even if the message had come in time, it is unlikely that Farnsworth's division would have had the energy to move. When the 32nd Division relieved part of the 91st and the 37th on a four-mile front, the guardsmen recovered sufficient pride and strength to march to the rear. Casualties totalled 3,460 men, but the division had taken 1,120 prisoners and twenty-three guns.

The 79th Division on the right of V Corps' bid for the western wing of Kriemhilde captured Montfaucon on 27th September. A regiment tried to flank Nantillois but was caught in full sight of the German defence works. Liaison with flanks was possible only by sending mounted messengers. Supply transport temporarily gave up the struggle to negotiate the Montfaucon road as the wreckage of vehicles hit by shells would only hinder the progress of road repair. Carrying parties brought food and other supplies three miles through the zone of shell-fire to the front. Regiments in reserve were alerted to clear the Beuge Wood of machine-gun nests and Nantillois on the main road on the right was occupied before noon on the third day. Given time to reform and a little rest, Oury's

*Above:* German prisoners pour in; some of them were deserters with Bolshevik sympathies. *Left:* A German plane brought down by American machine gunners northwest of Montfaucon. *Above right:* General Joseph T Dickman,

158th Brigade briefly penetrated Ogons Wood. The approach to the wood was made with the help of two tanks, both of which were disabled before the withdrawal. The Ogons Wood changed hands many times during the next seven days. Here at the foot of the heights, and two miles from the town of Cunel on the high ground, the German 236th Division blocked access to the Kriemhilde Line with great determination. Although weakened by the transfer of four battalions to the Aire, this division established a defensive line from Gesnes through the Cunel and Ogons Woods to the Brieulles Wood east of Nantillois. Two more attacks on the 29th on Ogons Wood, conducted under plunging machine-gun fire from the heights, were unsuccessful. On that first Sunday the divisional front moved forward only 300 yards. From the sky above the southern slopes of Kriemhilde spotters in a German balloon methodically directed fire on Americans in the ravines and on the slopes out of sight of ground observers. By the next day the energy and resources of Kuhn's men from the Atlantic coast were expended. Also relieving units of the 4th Division now in Brieulles Wood, Buck's regular 3rd Division moved in on the ridge along the northern edge of the Beuge Wood to a point 300 yards north of Nantillois.

The regular 3rd, which met its baptism of fire under Dickman on the Marne, marched northwards to the front in column along the Montfaucon road under shell-fire. The line from Beuge Wood to Nantillois was exposed to constant harassing fire. Out front were three bare ridges with hills and woods protecting the German left flank. On the third ridge was the Mamelle trench, a part of the Kriemhilde Line. On 3rd October Marwitz reinforced the Fifth Army with the 28th Reserves drawn originally from districts in Baden. Backed by an enlarged artillery brigade the 3rd – sometimes called the Marne Division – blanketed the first ridge with a heavy preparation. On 2nd October Buck's infantry ran forward in a series of rushes, stopping only to close gaps made in their ranks by machine-gun fire. A smoke screen assisted the morning advance, which carried Sladen's 5th Brigade across the first ridge under flank fire from Hill 250. An attempt to encircle Hill 250 by Hunt's 6th Brigade on the right was defeated by fire from Cunel Wood.

The following day the infantry was driven back from the second ridge by two field guns and machine-gunners firing at point-blank range. Another artillery barrage was put down on this ridge and the Mamelle trench in the rear. As part of the army attack on the 4th the Marne Division flanked by the 32nd on the left and the 80th on the right continued in its effort to drive a wedge into Kriemhilde in co-ordination with the 1st Division in the Aire valley. The barrier-gate to the Mamelle trench was controlled from Cunel Wood. One wave of infantry after another was repelled by the perimeter defences of the wood, but when the first troops broke in they found that internal paths were blocked with more machine-guns. Obliged to hide in fox-holes, the American regulars withdrew in small parties under the cover of darkness. The second ridge was stormed successfully on 5th October. During 7th/8th October Buck's division dug in along a front obliquely facing the Cunel heights from northwards towards Gesnes and running south of Hill 250 almost to the road leading up the hill to the town of Cunel. The opposing trenches were just seventy-five yards apart.

After their encouraging advance of seven miles on the first day, Hines' 4th Division pushed through the Brieulles Wood to the Nantillois – Brieulles road against increasing resistance. On the left this division helped the 79th in the capture of Nantillois; but was also repulsed from Ogons Wood and failed again to penetrate Fays Wood. As the front was narrowing with the course of the Meuse, the division's right rested in the woods to the west bank of the river. Enemy flank fire was concealed not only on the river bank, but also along the Meuse canal that follows the course of the river. Both field and heavy artillery were in range from the slopes of the Meuse heights and the infamous Borne de Cornouiller (Hill 378). The town of Brieulles on the division's right flank in the river bend held batteries of guns and surrounding swamps were defended by machine-gun nests. The division's line of advance was chosen along a path through Fays Wood northwards along the eastern edge of the Cunel heights to the Bois de Forêt. Before the general attack on 4th October the 80th (Blue Ridge) Division, which had been squeezed out of their sector, re-entered the line on the left of the 4th Division. With their left flank exposed at Ogons Wood, which the Blue Ridge men could not take after repeated charges, Hines' regular troops cleared the Fays Wood of machine-gun nests. The increasing volume of fire from every direction was a warning that Marwitz would not readily allow the Kriemhilde Line to be outflanked by a flying column moving at pace along the west bank of the river. Retiring during the night, the leading brigade fell back on Ville-aux-Bois farm, which they held against three counterattacks by the 5th Bavarian Reserves and under shell-fire directed against Fays Wood. On the 9th the tactical plan required that the men mark time until the 80th had caught up with them.

After probing north of Dannevoux Cronkhite's (Blue Ridge) Division occupied high ground alongside the 4th Division on the left in the area of the Bois de la Côte Lémont before being withdrawn to the Corps reserve. Moving back into line on 3rd October near Ogons Wood, the division was ready to play its part in the second great attack of the offensive on the following day. With the 159th Brigade (Lieutenant-Colonel Buchanan) in action, the Blue Ridge men relieved units of the 3rd on the left and of the 4th now on the right. Attacking throughout their first day across flank fire from both Cunel and Fay Woods, the brigade was no more successful than its predecessors in breaking into the Ogons Wood. Divisional artillery was ordered to concentrate all its guns on the area, and the Rhinelanders of the 236th Division were subjected to a gas attack. Overrunning the wood on the second day it changed hands several times in the next twenty-four hours. That night the wood was retaken by the 236th after the regimental commander regrouped the 459th Infantry Regiment and personally led his men back into their old position. Blue Ridge patrols infiltrating the northern end of the wood on the third day brought back valuable able information about what was in store from the next counterattack. The wood was bombarded again by the artillery brigade and machine-gun companies using Browning Heavies sent streams of bullets over the heads of the infantry making renewed attacks. On 6th October Brett's 160th Brigade was brought up in replacement and Ogons Wood was finally cleared, the brigade going on through the western parts of Fays and Malaumont Woods. Two days later the 80th moved into line with the 4th Division. On 9th October the American First Army was scheduled to make a general assault on the main line Kriemhilde defences.

After its brilliant swinging movement through Forges Wood to the Meuse, the usefulness of Bell's division west of the river was expended. Transferred to French XVII Corps (Claudel) the Illinois men chose to join Morton's 29th (National Guard) Division coming up on the Heights of the Meuse the hard way. While the divisional artillery provided a poor answer to the long-range heavies on the Borne de Cornouiller, the engineers wearing gas masks started building wooden bridges at Brabant and Consenoye. (Two days before furtive parties of the same engineers had made a thorough job of blowing up the existing river bridges.) When word came on the 29th that Morton's 'Blue and Grey' Division held the opposite bank, a regiment from the 33rd rushed from Forges Wood under heavy fire and made a crossing in broad daylight. A system of hills extending from the Verdun forts to the Borne de Cornouiller form the walls of a bowl. The slopes are wooded and cut by ravines commanding the bottom of the bowl itself, which is irregular, but everywhere in view of the heights. The 29th was to drive straight for the Borne de Cornouiller. Upon its success depended the success of the 33rd's consolidation on the east bank of the Meuse. After hot work at close quarters, the Blues and Greys captured Malbrouck hill, which was a strongpoint in the German support trench system of Verdun days. Then passing over open country under increasing German gunfire, they overran all the machine-gun nests in the dense Consenoye Wood. Now fully awake to XVII Corps' ambitious plan, Marwitz unleashed a torrent of gas shells from the heights on the rim of the bowl which was not to cease for three weeks. Bringing reserves across the river, Bell's 33rd advanced at heavy cost to the ridge east of Sivry, right under the guns of that towering Hill 378 or the Borne de Cornouiller.

As the American First Army was committed to continuous attacks, the replacement of men became a problem of vital importance. Casualties since 26th September had grown to nearly 75,000. In addition some 70,000 soldiers were treated in hospital for influenza during the same period, many of these cases developing into pneumonia, and the death rate from influenza rose to thirty-two per cent of cases for the AEF. The necessity to keep units in the line without the normal withdrawal period for rest and refitting led to the strength of the infantry company being reduced from 250 to 175 men. Nevertheless, the broadening of the front of attack to the east of the Meuse made it advisable to establish another army. Accordingly on 12th October the American Second Army was formed under General Bullard from troops then on the front extending from Fresnes-en-Woëvre to the Moselle. The American First Army was assigned to General Hunter Liggett, and new corps commanders

*Above:* 'A' Battery of 108th Field Artillery in action near Varennes. *Above right:* Gas mask drill. *Below:* The funeral of a fallen American soldier

**German dismounted cavalry on the march**

were appointed. At Ligny-en-Barrois General Pershing, as Commander of a group of armies, retained immediate command of the First Army until 16th October. Claudel's French XVII Corps east of the Meuse was under the direction of the First Army. Bullard's Second Army did not advance across the Woëvre in the general direction of the Briey iron basin until 5th November. When this advance took place French XVII Corps was in line with IV and VI Corps (latter Menoher). But General Pershing's concern on 9th October was to tighten the clamps on the Romagne and Cunel heights and then drive on to the Hindenburg Position with the maximum strength of the American First Army.

On 9th October the German Fifth Army, which was to suffer 25,000 casualties in the second and third weeks of October, was in a confident mood. Since 4th October the Group Meuse-West had in the centre held a superior opponent at bay. Although gun crews were showing signs of exhaustion, artillery batteries along the Kriemhilde Line remained unmolested. American air squadrons, which had concentrated on disrupting communications behind the lines, were ordered to patrol in close support of ground troops and in liaison with their corps artillery brigades. In the first two weeks of the offensive German planes had much their own way over the battle area, taking a heavy toll of American observation balloons. When remnants of the two Prussian divisions were withdrawn after Châtel-Chérery, von Kleist's Group Argonne consisted in part of the 52nd, 15th Bavarian and 240th Divisions. These formations blocked the Fléville gap from the environs of Cornay through St Juvin to Grandpré. Of these divisions only the Bavarians stayed in the line thoughout October. The Swabian Territorials of the 2nd *Landwehr* and the 37th Divisions were lodged at the entrance to the gap. Along the Romagne heights were the 115th and (at Bantheville) the 236th Divisions. The 13th from Westphalia (reduced to 200 men by 11th November) was also stationed in the neighbourhood of Bantheville

Wood. The 3rd Prussian Guard Division, arriving in trucks at Romagne from west of the Argonne, offered the stiffest resistance of the offensive. The 45th (Pomeranian) Reserves were located forward of the Romagne heights near the Fléville gap.

Covering the junction of Group Argonne and von Oven's Group Meuse-West the depleted 7th was next to the 41st Reserves and part of the 13th Division. On the Cunel heights the core of the Meuse-West group comprised the 107th, 88th and 28th Reserves. Until 25th October the Saxonian 123rd was also on Cunel and the 228th was moved across from Cunel to the Woëvre in mid-October. The

**A German heavy gun fires across the Meuse valley from a position on the high ground north of Verdun**

5th Bavarians defended Brieulles on the west bank of the Meuse. The 228th took post in Group Meuse-East alongside the Austro-Hungarian 1st (*Kaiserlich und Königliche*) Division and three German divisions of the Fifth Army. On their left completing cover of the front held by French XVII, II (Colonial) and American IV Corps was Group Beaumont numbering two divisions. Group Ornes on the eastern flank of *Heeresgruppe Gallwitz*, which extended to Abaucourt twelve miles north-east of Verdun, possessed four German and four Austro-Hungarian (*K und K*) Divisions. The three groups on General von Gallwitz's left flank were commanded by Austrian Lieutenant Field Marshal Metzger.

Gouraud's French Fourth Army operating a little distance west of the Argonne Forest, which had gone into the offensive almost simultaneously with the American First Army on 26th September, had been held up at Mont Blanc. The Marine Brigade of the 2nd Division (Lejeune USMC) with French tanks on 3rd October stormed and captured the enemy position on the Médéah Farm – Mont Blanc Ridge. The marines continued to advance and five days later took St Etienne with the help of Smith's 36th Division.

**A joke during gas mask drill**

The American 369th Infantry (French 161st Division) and the 371st and 372nd Infantry (French 157th Division) took part in the attack. The negro enlisted men fought alongside black African troops of French IX Corps from Morocco and French West African colonies. These three regiments were withdrawn with their divisions after crossing the Hindenburg Line on 8th October. First Lieutenant George Robb of the 369th Regiment won a

Medal of Honor at Séchault during 29th/30th September after his platoon came under heavy machine-gun fire and he himself was severely wounded. In spite of his wounds he established outposts during the night and was again wounded by a shell-burst that also killed his senior company officers. Leading the company beyond the town and clearing machine-gun nests on the way, the advance secured the battalion's hold on Séchault. On 13th October the Fourth Army crossed the Aisne at its confluence with the Aire five miles south-west of Grandpré. In an assault beginning on the following day, the French were to outflank the Germans on the Americans' left, while I Corps next in line held off the Group Argonne beyond Châtel-Chéréry and protected the flank of V Corps. V and III Corps would drive salients through the Kriemhilde Line along the flanks of the Romagne and Bantheville Woods, intending to clear out the woods between the salients and push north.

The ability of the 'Liberty' Division (the 77th) to take advantage of the successes on both flanks had started the withdrawal of the Germans from the Argonne Forest. After the relief of their encircled troops in forward areas the men pressed on impatiently to the Grandpré gap at the northern tip of the ridge. They met with only desultory machine-gun fire and occasional concentrations of shell-fire on open spaces. On the 10th the division advanced four miles in formation and forward patrols, encountering no resistance, emerged from the forest into the open facing the gap. Beyond the Aire as it turns westwards through the gap below Grandpré the naturally strong positions on the northern bank of the river culminated in the Heights of Grandpré. Near the bend of the river the village of St Juvin was near the western end of the fragmentary trench system of the Kriemhilde Line. With the First Army poised to strike at Kriemhilde proper on 14th October, the 77th swung to the right across swampy ground towards St Juvin to relieve pressure on the centre of the corps front. Expecting an attack from the south, the defenders of St Juvin were taken by surprise when one of the American battalions crossed the river and entered the village from the east. The movement from the west was intended as no more than a threat, but the leading battalion in its eagerness raced into the attack. Unhappily stumbling into a barrage laid southwards along the expected line of advance this battalion suffered heavily, eight officers being killed and twenty wounded before St Juvin fell later the same day.

The small town of Grandpré lies back against the escarpment which protrudes from the Bourgogne Wood, and commanded the northern bank of the river and the narrow opening of

**Machine gunners at Grandpré**

the Aire valley. The Germans had covered the approaches to the town with artillery, trench mortars and machine-guns. No movement in daylight in the open was possible without being seen by observers in the town, and patrols infiltrating across the river through a ford encountered a brusque reception. With full support from their artillery brigade, Johnson's 154th Infantry Brigade led the assault on Grandpré on the following night. While a battalion rushed the ford, detachments crossed the river by boat-bridges and others waded into the water and swam to the opposite bank. All night fire plunged down on the intruders from the heights, and raking fire from the houses swept the streets. Although the 1st Battalion of the 307th Infantry made a firm *logement* in the southern part of the town, the job of evicting the Germans from Grandpré fell on the 16th to McRae's 78th Division. The 'Liberty' men had been in action for nearly three weeks, and all but five days of that time had been spent in the Argonne Forest. Now the forest welcomed them back as jubilant troops streamed into the rest camps and hide-outs built with such thoroughness for the rehabilitation and comfort of the German army. Kleist had moved north from his well-appointed headquarters to Buzancy, leaving behind these excellent facilities for General Alexander and his staff. But the division was only rested for fifteen days. At the end of the month the 77th re-entered the line at Hill 182 north of St Juvin and joined in the pursuit of the enemy northwards to the Meuse.

Named the 'Lightning' Division, McRae's draft men came mainly from New Jersey, Pennsylvania and New York State. Newly arrived from the Limey sector north of Toul in Lorraine, the division had earlier trained with the British First Army in Flanders; but the epic struggle for the heights of Grandpré was quite unlike anything so far experienced by the men during their three months in France. Establishing contact with the French 71st Division on the left and the 82nd on the right, the 'Lightning' Division held the line from Grandpré in the west to the southern perimeter of Loges Wood a little over a mile further east. Effective liaison with the French was at first impractical as the Bourgogne Wood – a bastion commanding the approach of Gouraud's right flank in its movement to Sedan – created a barrier between the French and American forces. On the right on more high ground the outpost of Loges Wood, which is about a mile in breadth and depth, barred passage east of the Grandpré heights in the direction of Buzancy. At the time of the army attack on 14th October the importance of holding the American left at Grandpré was equal to that of holding the right on the Meuse heights. Moreover violent pressure from both flanks was necessary to draw enemy forces from the centre of the Kriemhilde Line. In Grandpré the principal street of the town runs up the hill against the western slope of the escarpment. Machine-gunners and snipers could come and go from the heights into the back doors of the houses and shoot at will from upstairs windows. The high ground above the town was crowned by the ruins of an old fortress with stone walls which had to be scaled. The only possible way to attack this position was over a narrow causeway. Known to the 78th as 'the Citadel', the Germans owed the apparent security of this defensive position to the French well-to-do of the middle ages and their fears of rebellion amongst the peasants of Grandpré.

Hersey's left-hand brigade took the town after two days of house-to-house fighting; reserves crossing the river under heavy fire from the heights. The *Landwehr* troops fell back to the Citadel and also beyond to a park that extends for about 500 yards. Beyond that Talma hill, Hill 180, Hill 204 and Bellejoyeuse Farm formed a rampart of heights at the edge of the Bourgogne Wood. On the 19th the Lightnings made the assault on the Citadel. Two separate parties attempted to scale the walls of the fortress. During the American bombardment German guns in the area were dropped for safety into deep dugouts. As soon as the firing was over the guns were hoisted up by cable and turned on the advancing infantry. A shower of bombs came down on the heads of the first scaling party, and although the second party reached the top, the men were repulsed by machine-gun fire. The infantry had everywhere to fall back, and four days went by before a lieutenant and four men finally scaled a wall under a powerful rolling barrage and rushed forward to Bellejoyeuse Farm. Two waves of infantry followed, but they were obliged to fall back to the northern edge of the park. Jumping-off places having been gained, progress became more rapid in a series of thrusts. On the 25th one party entered the Bourgogne Wood, having taken Talma hill. The brigade was unfortunately arranged and a gap of half-a-mile existed between the troops in the park and in the wood. The men held on for two days under severe bombardment while other units fought to eliminate machine-gun nests and snipers and close the gap. When Bellejoyeuse Farm was taken Hills 180 and 204 had already been stormed with the help of the French coming up on the left. After fourteen days of bitter fighting the 78th was firmly established on the Grandpré heights.

Dean's right-hand brigade situated half-way between Grandpré and St Juvin crossed the river on the 16th, and plunged through mud knee-deep on the opposite bank in the face of a blaze of fire from the Loges Wood. Completely exposed, the men who reached the edge of the wood were half-way through by the following morning. The attackers from the west dug in on the west side of the wood; but the choice before them was to go forward, go back or be massacred in their fox-holes. The wood was thick enough to conceal artillery and sparse enough to give machine-guns free play. In the wood machine-gun nests were placed in the first defence line at intervals of forty yards. In the depths of the wood guns were sited to trap the infantry in interlocking fields of fire.

On the morning of the 18th support battalions passed through the first line on to the high ground, each unit clearing its way as fast as it could. With some men penetrating to the northern part of the wood, the attack developed into a fight between individuals as well as between small groups. When the Germans gassed the southern edge of the wood to force back reserves the Americans in the wood fell back. On 20th October the brigade was ordered back to the Grandpré – St Juvin road. But the brigade had in fact used up all its reserves and the division had none available. The exhausted men in the gas-saturated Loges Wood complained when they were told to pull back. By this time the Germans had the wood encircled by machine-gunners, and on the far left they still held the escarpment and Citadel at Grandpré. The brigade retreated under crossfire from the machine-guns and a shower of gas and high-explosive shells. Suffering 5,234 casualties, twelve days went by before McRae's division went back to the Loges Wood. But the consolidation of the division on the Grandpré heights and the breakthrough in the centre of the First Army front made a further attack in this area of less immediate importance.

When, on orders from Gallwitz, the 2nd *Landwehr* withdrew on 7th October to the Aire, Châtel-Chéhéry lay forward in a salient extending from the Aire gap between Cornay and Fléville. After Lindsey's 164th Brigade took Châtel-Chéhéry and Corporal York became better-known than his divisional commander, General Duncan hastily ordered up Cronin's 163rd Brigade from the corps reserve. The division went without sleep however

*Above :* A German machine gun position which held up the Americans near Grandpré
*Below :* 170mm *minenwerfer* (mine thrower) in action

until the evening of 10th October finally saw the capture of Cornay and the culmination of the movement in the trough of the Aire. The town of Cornay was defended by non-commissioned officers and machine-gunners who could be relied upon to fight to the death. But draft men – many rejected on enlistment by another American division because they were too small and grossly undernourished – gained and lost Cornay three times before remnants of the *Landwehr* and 45th Reserves were put to flight. West of the so-called Châtel hill Swabian Territorials repelled all assaults. In the first approach to Cornay and the heights to the west, roving German field guns fired point-blank at the waves of advancing infantry. Although in places the men could climb only by drawing themselves up by the bushes and dwarf trees, a reserve regiment of Lindsey's brigade on the left gallantly forced its way on to the high ground. Repeated counterattacks from Fléville towards Châtel-Chéhéry a mile or so due south of Cornay, did not deflect the division from its task of taking Cornay and advancing beyond the Aire gap east of St Juvin.

Although a regiment of the 45th Reserves made a spirited attack on Châtel hill, the German troops were generally speaking too exhausted for assault tactics. But after Lindsey's brigade was driven out of Cornay after house-to-house fighting on the 8th, *Landwehr* troops infiltrating from the heights created havoc in the American ranks regrouping in the valley at the foot of the Argonne ridge. American field gunners attached to the infantry were encouraged to use the German tactics of firing at the enemy on their own initiative over open sights. Back in Cornay a second and third time on the following day the 82nd was twice evicted. On one occasion Colonel Mayer assembled what was left of his regiment of the 45th Reserves and – exposed to fire from Hotchkiss machine-gunners – led a sortie through the village; the colonel personally capturing two American lieutenants and 164 enlisted men lodged temporarily in the village houses. The second assault of the day was broken up by a lone German field gun, which continued to fire throughout the engagement. The two officers who manned the gun were all that was left of an

entire regiment of artillery. After the fall of Cornay on the 10th troops on the heights on the left went on to capture Marcq a mile south of the Grandpré – St Juvin road. Passage through the Aire gap proved a nightmare for the centre battalions following the winding course of the river. On the right a regiment crossed the river and, relieving troops of the 1st Division, occupied Sommerance on high ground on the edge of the

ted by artillery. On the left at that time Cronin's brigade was well ahead and across the trenches in front of the prepared defensive position. Patrols searched up and down the river below St Juvin in darkness and in vain for a ford; and called for engineers to build a foot bridge. At dawn machine-gunners concentrated with deadly accuracy on infantry rushing the bridge, but elements of two companies got across and threw a ring

Romagne heights.

When forward troops along the river were riddled with casualties, the second line 'leap-frogged' and charged into the machine-gun fire. One battalion had all its commissioned officers killed or so badly wounded that they could not move; another lost all officers but one. The division reached Kriemhilde at 0800 hours on the 11th, but was immediately exposed to crossfire from machine-guns suppor-

around St Juvin. The brigade was across the river in strength the following day and heading for high ground north and north-east of the village. In the general offensive of the 14th the centre of the division touched on Kriemhilde near the river bend west of Châtillon ridge. Sweeping over Hill 182 the left took the commanding positions which let the 77th into St Juvin; and the 82nd persisted in attacking on this sector in support of the Lightnings' effort at Loges Wood. The centre and right-hand regiments went on finally just a mile beyond Sommerance in flank support of the Rainbow Division storming Châtillon ridge on the right. On the 21st General Duncan consolidated his position here in the area of Ravin aux Pierres. With 6,764 casualties but effective rifle strength down to 4,700 men, the general set up local medical posts to rehabilitate slightly gassed, wounded and sick men, and was able by these means to hold the line until the end of the month. The war was over for the men of the 82nd Division.

In driving the wedge to Fléville and the taking of Montrefagne, the 1st Division was badly shaken up. Now under Corps new direction, over a third of the riflemen had fallen, and German artillery hurled gas shells at woods where reserves might take cover. Reinforced by a roving brigade of the 91st Division, Summerall's doctrine was never to give ground taken uphill. His drive from the northern outskirts of Fléville to clear the eastern wall of the Aire was hindered variously by heavy rain, fog and murderous fire from across the valley. A scarcity of supplies was due to the accurate shelling of American transport in the rear. Along the entire Corps front depleted German divisions intermingled as they retreated to the

**American field gun position**

Kriemhilde Line. The East Prussians of the 37th Division counter-attacked again and again near Fléville; but the 52nd had few effectives left after the fierce engagement and gassing at Exermont at the foot of Hill 240 on the Romagne heights. American artillery was increasing in efficiency every day. The 115th succumbed to pressure after

**German and American wounded at a Red Cross dressing station**

annihilating fire had broken through their ranks and went back to Romagne Wood. Throwing engineers and every spare man into the battle, the division passed through this wood on the 10th and met the 82nd at Sommerance. At this point the outlying defences of the Kriemhilde Line were no more than a mile away. After constant probing of the enemy positions, it was decided on the 12th that a breakthrough could only be made by fresh troops. Casualties since 1st October had mounted to 8,554 dead and wounded. Although the artillery was left in the line what remained of the infantry returned in faultlessly good order to the I Corps reserve, and did not see action again until the push for the Freya Position on 1st November and the breakout from the Argonne.

Menoher, who had commanded the 42nd (Rainbow) Division since earliest days in Lorraine, put his two infantry brigades into line along the northern edge of the Romagne Wood on the eve of the general offensive. On the 14th the left brigade (Lenihan) attacked towards St Georges and the right brigade (MacArthur) commenced the ascent of the Châtillon ridge to the village of Landres. During the next three days the Rainbows – with the 82nd on the left and the 32nd on the right – fought one of the toughest actions of the Battle of the Argonne. German resistance was especially brave and veteran units of the Fifth Army made the most of positions as vital and well-prepared as they were naturally strong. On the left on the first day the few survivors of patrols pushing ahead along the southern slopes of Hill 288 were forced to crawl back to their start-line under a blanket of machine-gun fire. The thrust for St Georges with the aid of tanks on the second day struck the 15th Bavarians as they relieved the 37th Division. But as the stunned Bavarians fell back from the village, it was reoccupied by the former incumbents who repelled four massed attacks by Lenihan's brigade before nightfall. After taking Hill 242 and Hill 288, units of the brigade were badly gassed while cutting through intricate wire defences. After the Rainbows regrouped for a second time, the defenders of St Georges were unable to hold the invasion on the 16th and Lenihan began to consolidate most energetically on his sector west of the Châtillon ridge. His position was the safer because MacArthur's brigade had made the first breach in Kriemhilde along the line from the west, and was confidently in command of the high ground.

On the first day of the offensive the right brigade was held on the slippery ascent of the 1,000ft ridge, where German machine-gunners stood until they were killed or so badly wounded

**18th Infantry Regiment on the side of Hill 240 near Exermont**

that they could not man their guns. On the second day some of the National Guardsmen were on the top and clung to the ground after digging themselves into the rain-soaked earth. On the 16th units shattered during the climb were reorganised and reserves sent up the slope for the assault on Landres. East Prussian troops of the 41st Division fought desperately to stem the onslaught of massed waves of American riflemen. As the machine-gunners scattered the ranks of the guardsmen, the dwindling spirit of the German riflemen was rallied by the calmness of their comrades with the Maxims. Guardsmen drew their pistols and bayonets clashed in hand-to-hand combat. American artillery had done its work in Landres, and after the village was cleared MacArthur organised his positions on the high ground. The last counterattack

**German machine gunners braced the dwindling spirits of the riflemen**

**Bayonet practice** was driven back by the presence of mind of one soldier. As Private Neibaur, the sole survivor of an automatic rifle patrol, lay wounded in both legs about one hundred yards in front of the company's skirmish line, he saw lines of enemy infantry approaching. His action in killing four soldiers who bore down on him alerted his company, and the counterattack was promptly broken up with deadly fire. Although exposed to a hail of bullets from his own company, he continued to shoot Germans at close quarters until the attack was over. There was nothing further for the 42nd to do during the next two weeks except to make sure that its gains were not lost. The storming of the Châtillon ridge cost the Rainbows 2,895 casualties. After withdrawing from Gouraud's Fourth Army front and a brief period of training near Châlons the 2nd Division took over the sector on the night of 31st October.

So near to Kriemhilde on 8th October, the Arrows were determined to remain there while patrols probed the defensive position. Before the National Guard of Michigan and Wisconsin was to conquer the Dame Marie ridge and take Romagne going uphill through the gap between the Romagne and Cunel heights, the 32nd Division had to make preparation equal to the task. Haan's next move was closely connected with the 1st Division's costly operation driving that wedge across the western slope of the Romagne heights to Sommerance. On 9th October the brigade on loan from the 91st to this area assaulted Hill 255, and after capturing a concrete block-house on the reverse slope was soon established on the ridge in Veloup Wood. From this point on the divisional sector the defensive position stretched eastwards along the Dame Marie ridge and extended across the gap in front of the town of Romagne to the Cunel Wood. Shivering with cold and weakened by hunger

and fatigue, the new tenants of Veloup Wood held the link with the 1st under gas bombardment until McCoy's 63rd Infantry Brigade made the main assault on the ridge on their immediate right. Covered along the sector by the fire of three artillery brigades, the progress of the centre battalions across and beyond the left of Mamelle trench along the Romagne road was regulated by the speed of movement on both flanks. After penetrating Mamelle trench, Winans' 64th Infantry Brigade swung right west of Cunel Wood and encircled Romagne. During five days of street fighting neither side knew who was winning the battle for the small town. Fifth Army reports of having repeatedly driven the Americans out of Romagne indicate the severity of the fighting; but the Arrows made no claim to having captured the town until the army offensive of 14th October.

The 32nd's attack of the 14th was made in close concert with the Rainbows' assault on the Châtillon ridge. Some units of the left-hand brigade had clung to the forward slope for several days while others engaged in hand-to-hand fighting along the high ground. The intrusions on Kriemhilde on the ridge and at Mamelle trench had fully aroused the German gun crews and machine-gunners and the Arrows were lashed at every point along the line. The 123rd Division was moved forward to the ridge from Bantheville Wood, and the 236th Division counterattacked frequently across the Romagne road in the centre of the sector. When the 3rd Prussian Guard relieved the 115th Division in and further west of Romagne, the latter could not make good its escape from the line. At one stage of the fight for Romagne when the Prussians were breaking down, General Kreutzer advancing on foot at the head of the leading unit lead elements of the 115th and 236th through the town to a line 800 yards to the south. Meanwhile the 13th Division was moving down the road east of Bantheville Wood. On the 14th units still burrowing into the steep and slippery wall of the ridge were given a new lease of life when the 42nd eliminated flank fire from Hill 288. One battalion went swiftly around to the left and was not heard from again until the men climbed on to the ridge in triumph from the north side. By this time another regiment was on top from the south and the position was made secure. On the right Romagne fell finally to a flanking movement with the help of a flexible barrage. The Arrows had gone clean through the Kriemhilde Line!

Advancing along the eastern slope of the Romagne heights and the road which presently curls eastwards through Aincreville to the Meuse, the 32nd went through Chauvignon Wood and the eastern part of Romagne Wood. Wright's 89th Division, which had been in the corps reserve for about a week, took over the line on the 20th less than a mile north of Romagne town. Although the fighting in Bantheville Wood was not at first severe, the firing got worse as the draft men from Kansas and Missouri plodded on. The wood was gassed and the paths made impassable by rain and fallen trees. Stretcher-parties had to wade knee-deep in mud for a mile-and-a-half to bring back the wounded and other men sick with influenza. Over 4,000 men were pulled out during the 89th's stay in the line. At Gesnes, now situated almost four miles behind the front line, a bathing and disinfecting plant built by the Germans was put to good use during the influx of casualties. The division now dug in between the northern tip of Bantheville Wood along a line running south-eastwards to Rappes Wood on the northern slope of the Cunel heights. The position on the left at Bantheville Wood marked the most northerly point of the advance of Liggett's American First Army on 31st October. On taking over,

**Wounded receive treatment in a ruined church from an ambulance company in rear of 1st Division sector**

## Street fighting in Cunel

Summerall had been determined that V Corps would go through Kriemhilde at all costs. The front fell not far short of a line with Bantheville a few miles east at Aincreville, and then curled southwards around III Corps' zone of advance on the Cunel Heights before turning along the northern edge of Brieulles Wood to the Meuse.

On 8th October Buck's 3rd Division was not in control of Cunel Wood south-east of Mamelle trench. West of the wood a counterattack against Sladen's 5th Brigade approaching Hill 253 was halted by persistent fire from a disabled French tank. Private Barkley of Company K, 4th Infantry, had installed a captured enemy machine-gun in the tank. He opened fire as the first wave of riflemen came abreast of his post, and continued firing after the tank was hit by a shell from a 76mm gun. This action cleared the way for the brigade's capture of Hill 253. On the 9th the Cunel Wood was cleared of the enemy, and Hunt's 6th Brigade took on the major part of the Mamelle trench south-east of Romagne. Fierce fighting occurred on this sector until the 3rd was passed through by the 5th Division along the trench system on 13th October; but Buck's division remained on the offensive.

Meanwhile on the right below Cunel Cronkhite's 80th Division was engaged from 6th to 11th October in a series of attacks beyond the Ogons Wood. After racing to the Brieulles heights the Blue Ridge men had moved over to the left of the corps area. On the forward slope of the Cunel heights the Cunel Wood lies on the left and the Ogons Wood on the right of the road leading northwards from Nantillois to Cunel town. The division had only to repeat its successes of the first three days of the Argonne offensive and the troops would be in Cunel in a matter of hours. But there

**Major-General Buck. He took over 3rd Division from Dickman**

was no reason to believe that there were fewer machine-guns in the Ogons Wood than when the 79th had been repulsed. Stalemate had existed at Ogons for five days until Cronkhite on the 5th sent his waves of infantry across open ground to the wood's edge. The barrage of bullets from the Browning Heavies sent over the heads of the assailants in the charge led to the wood's seizure on that day.

In line with the 3rd the 'Blue Ridge' Division waited for the regulars to clear Cunel Wood before attempting a further advance, but did not attack until twelve hours after the assault on Mamelle trench on the left on 9th October. As the first wave of infantry advanced, the Germans dropped a curtain of gunfire in front of the second wave. The strongpoint at Ville-aux-Bois farm was overrun and the leading brigade reached the Cunel-Brieulles road. After dark two companies slipped quietly into Cunel and captured two complete battalion staffs. At dawn observers in the north and east noted the dangerously exposed positions of the 80th, and quickly passed word to the gunners. Two companies were decimated, two others scattered in confusion; but the 80th did not give up the idea of attack. Against a whirlwind of fire they managed to go beyond the Cunel – Brieulles road, but were unable to hold their positions. The road was a target line in the grey autumn light along which human figures were plainly visible to watchful gunners. On the 11th a brigade of the 5th Division relieved the 80th south of Cunel; but it was the 3rd moving eventually on the right of the 5th that advanced on this sector after clearing the Cunel Wood. Cunel town was entered by the 3rd soon afterwards but not completely cleared of Germans until the push of 14th October. From then on the salient across the Kriemhilde Line from Châtillon ridge to Brieulles Wood developed slowly but relentlessly. The defence works combined many of the advantages of the old trench system with facilities for the latest methods of open warfare upon chosen and very formidable terrain. With the 4th Division on the east of the Cunel heights III Corps (Hines promoted) took the lion's share of the Kriemhilde bulge that existed in late October and measured five miles in breadth and two miles in depth at Bantheville and Aincreville.

McMahon's 5th Division passed through the 3rd along the trench system at Mamelle on 13th October. Moving on the left of their fellow regulars of the 3rd, the 5th, whose emblem was the ace of diamonds, had already seen some action on the Cunel – Brieulles road. According to the plan the Aces were to advance across open ground in a corridor between the artillery fire of the Romagne heights and the flanking machine-gun nests of the Pultière and Rappes Woods. Progress along this path was unlikely however unless the advancing troops first stopped to silence the machine-guns in the Pultière Wood. The enemy's artillery fire struck the front and rear echelons of the 5th Division simultaneously, causing heavy losses. In the inevitable confusion the regulars scrambled over Hills 260 and 271 and down the slopes into an increasing volume of machine-gun fire in the valley below. On the crests of the hills the Aces were all but boxed in by long-range gunfire from three sides. The American batteries did not knock out the machine-gun nests in the Pultière and Rappes Woods. Moreover the light and medium guns were no answer to the heavy guns firing from the Borne de Cornouiller east of the Meuse. The Pultière Wood is about half the size of Rappes to the north. The latter is about a mile long and separated from the former by a narrow open space. On the 14th, part of Malone's 10th Infantry Brigade, passing under fire from Cunel town, was checked in the woods east of Pultière. Advancing further the following day, units dug in within yards of the opposing entrenchments. Battalions of four German divisions falling back from the vicinity of Cunel Wood were concentrated west of the town. Although the resistance of most of these units was impaired by enormous losses, the 123rd which met the 3rd Division at Cunel was in comparatively good shape.

With Castner's brigade on the left the rush for Pultière resulted in some formations bursting through and reaching the northern edge of the Rappes Wood. With no support battalions available McMahon ordered the troops back. Although the small band was holding its own with snipers in Rappes, the men retraced their steps over the ground they had won past the bodies of their dead comrades. On the 17th when Ely took over the Aces, rifle strength was reported at 3,316 men; but Hills 260 and 271 and Pultière Wood had to be held at any price.

On the 20th the division concentrated all its available men for another attempt on the Rappes Wood. Following up a heavy barrage the Aces made swift work of taking the wood the next day. At 1800 hours the enemy counterattacked, but American artillery repelled the infantry with a barrage lasting only three minutes. The 90th Division relieved the 5th in the Rappes Wood on 22nd October. On the right the 3rd Division (now Preston Brown) was still going strong. Moving earlier in liaison and lending artillery support to the 5th's advance on Rappes, the 3rd now went for Clairs Chênes Wood and Hill 299 in deadly earnest. Failing in the latter objective, General Brown converged two attacks upon Hills 299 and 297. These two important vantage points for observers in the Argonne were won and the line straightened with professional precision. A violent bombardment of the Clairs Chênes forced an American machine-gun battalion and engineers to withdraw. A Yankee regimental commander rallied all the stragglers he could find, and led them in a charge which drove the Germans from the wood, and re-established the line. German guns pounded Hill 299; and the regulars repelled two attempts to take this valuable position.

On the night of the 26th the 3rd was relieved by the 5th Division. In the line for twenty-six days the 3rd paid its price in blood for taking the Mamelle trench and enduring the crossfire on the western slopes of the Cunel heights. 8,422 casualties amounted to two-thirds of the infantry strength of the 3rd Division. The regulars resumed the advance on 17th November in comfort: by rail via Remich in Luxembourg through the Rhineland, arriving in Mayen near Koblenz three weeks later.

Allen's 90th Division drawn from Oklahoma and Texas moved up from the Puvenelle sector elsewhere in Lorraine. When they took over in Rappes Wood the offensive had slowed down. The final attack in October included the occupation of certain 'jumping-off' places. With the 89th on the left the 90th sprang from Rappes Wood and captured the village of Bantheville on 23rd October. The next day the division drove ahead until it reached Freya, the fourth line of the Hindenburg defences in the Argonne. The Freya was not as strong as Kriemhilde and not in fact a continuous system of trenches. Strong machine-gun emplacements were supported by fragments of trenches. An attack on Freya was not part of the immediate plan. Ordered to dig in near Aincreville, vigilant patrols were on the alert for counterattacks. Under cross artillery fire the men prepared for the next offensive with gas masks on their faces. As elsewhere along the front to Bantheville Wood troops were constantly harassed by gas bombardment.

In numerous attacks during the period 4th-12th October the 4th Division captured Fays Wood and went on to take a line of woods along the eastern slope of the Cunel heights. The 'Bulldog' Division was pounded all along the way by medium and heavy batteries firing from the east bank of the Meuse. The town of Brieulles, which is surrounded by swamps in the bend of the river, was by-passed in the advance. At night machine-gunners in Brieulles swept fields of human targets revealed by the light of bursting shells from the Borne de Cornouiller. Barrages of gas shells were laid across the path of advance and into the woods ahead. The Bulldogs knew as they pressed forward that their own artillery could not match the fury of the enemy fire. Elements of four German divisions of Group Meuse West were stationed on the eastern slopes of Cunel. Tiers of machine-gun nests pointed eastwards to the Meuse river and canal. Relieved on 18th October by the 5th Division, the Bulldogs had spent twenty-three days in the welter of fire on the Meuse littoral. After their advance of eight miles on the first day all enemy positions had been taken by frontal attack. The 4th lost 6,000 officers and men dead and wounded, but captured 2,731 prisoners and forty-four guns.

The Kriemhilde breakthrough was accelerated when Gallwitz withdrew the left wing of Group Meuse-West to the Bantheville – Aincreville – Cléry line. During the second and third weeks of October alone the Fifth Army reported 24,928 casualties and 7,887 men missing. While III Corps consolidated on the Cunel heights, elements of the 4th Division remaining in the line fell back behind Brieulles to the heights of the same name. The Battle of the Argonne was over by 31st October, but apart from the devastating flank fire from the Meuse heights, units fighting east of the river had their influence on the progress of the American First Army through the Argonne. Indeed the dispositions of the Allied armies on the Western Front in late October and Ludendorff's defiant hopes of defending the line of the Meuse suggested to Gallwitz that the *coup de grâce* might

**German 7·7mm guns fall into American hands**

yet be delivered by a full-scale offensive across the Woëvre plain. German resistance in the Argonne was weakened by the deployment of reinforcements on the left wing of the German Fifth Army. The vulnerability of the right flank of III Corps west of the river is explained by the lack of progress in the face of heavy odds on the Meuse heights. By the end of October the advance had no more than touched on the second Hindenburg position south of Sivry. French XVII Corps at that time was on a line five miles back from III Corps' positions on the Cunel heights, and a mile or so in the rear of the 4th Division south of Brieulles.

After the swing to the river, Bell's 33rd Division was about to undertake a far more difficult manoeuvre. On the 9th Pershing had begun to take the threat of the Borne de Cornouiller more realistically. Claudel's corps was to make a drive from the start-line of the German Verdun offensive of 1916 at Samogneux. Morton's 29th Division was to push straight for the towering heights; but progress on the first day depended largely on Bell's ability to get all his men across the river at Brabant and Consenoye. The 33rd's pivotal function demanded rapid assembly for the advance on the river bank. The French 18th Division, which at first occupied this position, now moved over and the French 26th Division was on the far right. The battle opened when the Austrian 5th Regiment of Infantry, stationed adjacent to the Meuse, received the shock of an American mass attack under cover of the morning fog. After losing an observation point known to them as Crown Prince hill, a counter attack by German troops blocked further advance that day. Bringing more reserves across the river the 33rd actually reached the ridge east of Sivry right under the guns of the Borne de Cornouiller. On their right the 29th charged again and again for the possession of the Plat-Chêne ravine, which was swept by plunging fire from left and right and saturated with gas. Casualties were enormous on both sides. The slaughter on Sivry ridge was justified only by the number of shells III Corps was spared from receiving on the left. As the left flank had to hold the river bank, the 33rd entrenched in the Dans-les-Vaux valley through the Chaume Wood. Now along the sector wilting Austrian troops were being replaced by veterans from Prussia and Württemburg, who could be relied upon to meet attacks with counterattacks. New troops now arriving here amounted altogether to five divisions.

Away from the river bank the 32nd Division mounted a counterattack on the 10th from Etraye to recover ground lost by the Austrians the previous day. In the evening the German line stretched from Sivry eastwards through Ormont and Haumont Woods to Flabas. The fighting at close quarters was especially severe in Haumont Wood. The Borne de Cornouiller is about three miles from the Meuse. Southwards in the direction of the attack it slopes down into the

A soldier of the Yankee Division from New England writes a letter home from a ruined village east of the Meuse

steep-walled ravine of the Vaux de Mille Mais. The eastern end of the ravine gives way to a series of ridges rising to the summit of Hill 370, which protected the Grande Montagne Wood and was flanked by Hill 378. Thence an encircling ridge turns southwards to Verdun. With geographical features resembling a bowl the defensive positions (Giselhur Line) were reinforced with concrete pillboxes on the crests and forward slopes. The approach of the two American divisions was covered by small interlocking and wooded hills and ridges cut by ravines. The supply line along the main road near the river bank was strafed by gunfire by night and day. The French line of advance from Samogneux ran through an area of villages ruined by bombardment in the Verdun battles, through woods and fields of shell-craters. In an area of desolation troops rested in rat-infested and odorous dugouts roofed by débris from the villages. Transport was halted until shell-torn cars, motor-trucks and dead horses were removed from the roadways and new craters filled in by the engineers. Engineers at work were constantly under fire along the entire sector. The Corps operation had to be fan-shaped; concentration in any given area meant annihilation.

The 33rd held off counterattacks and continued to nag the enemy on the slopes of the Borne de Cornouiller until relieved on 21st October by the French 15th Colonials. The 33rd was under orders to attempt no advance; but in the east the 29th (The Blues and Greys) was forcing the action among the ravines and woods of the Molleville farm region. With French regiments overlapping the American sector, the front line and its support positions were being continually gassed. The Austrian 1st and Saxonian 32nd fought very stubbornly in the centre of the sector. Sivry changed hands several times. Along the line of the 15th Division no less than five American attacks were repulsed.

Ormont Wood rose to the crest of Hill 360, which commanded the southern side of the road and approaches to the Borne de Cornouiller. On the other side of the road are the Reine and Chênes Woods. Beyond these lies Belleu Wood, on the same side of the road. On the 12th Morton's Division co-operated with the French in trying to take the key points at Ormont and Belleu after an encircling movement. Following repeated charges, the Blues and Greys reached the edge of Ormont Wood. There they looked up the slope through the thickets to the summit of Hill 360. On the north side of the road Reine and part of Chêne Woods were taken in spite of counterattacks. On the 15th the attack was developed towards Molleville farm on the left and Grande Montagne on the right. Much ground was gained on the left and some on the right, where the fire from the Etraye ridge stopped the advance.

The wooded terrain at Ormont prevented the defenders from getting a clear view of their assailants. But artillery and machine-gun fire plunging indiscriminately down the slope halted the advance of the 29th and they were unable to hold any ground so far gained. After the encircling movement was complete Captain Blohm fought his way out of Ormont with his battalion; and regained possession after rallying the remnants of two companies. At Haumont Wood a German battalion was decimated by an American bombardment. Further east at Flabas a surprise attack supported by tanks was repulsed by Territorials from Schleswig-Holstein. Five French tanks were blown up in the attack. The Corps front was comparatively quiet on 17th October, but German infantry regained some ground lost on the flanks the previous day. The Blues and Greys continued to harass until the National Guardsmen tried to break through in the general direction of Etraye – Damvillers on 23rd October. The attempt failed when the troops came under the fire of artillery and *minenwerfers* of the 228th Division. After a number of attacks on the right had failed on the line of the 32nd, the 29th fell back to Etraye hill. Renewed American thrusts were repelled by counterattacks, and an attempt to roll up the enemy line from an easterly direction met with failure, so strong was the resistance of the 102nd Saxonian Infantry Regiment. The 1st *Landwehr* now joined in the fight moving in from north of Flabas.

Relieving the French 18th Division south-west of Flabas the 26th (Yankee) Division (now Cole) attacked on the morning of the 23rd. In line with the Blues and Greys the New Englanders made an ambitious assault on Etraye ridge. As soon as it was known that the ridge attack was succeeding they put in a reserve battalion at Belleu Wood. These were bold tactics, for just over the crest beyond Belleu the slope runs down to the plain of the Woëvre. During the course of a savage reception the battalion swept over the machine-guns and through the wood. Batteries whose fire had been the curse of III Corps swung and concentrated on that exposed patch of woods. The Yankees had to withdraw from the wood during the night, which was lit up by the fury of bursting shells. They fought throughout the following day for both Belleu Wood and Ormont Wood (Hill 360). A smoke-screen protected the first entry into Belleu, when they advanced 500 yards. The Germans drew back from their advanced line of fox-holes to their strong shell-proof emplacements, and called for a barrage to blast the charge. The machine-gunners in the pill boxes and log-covered *abattis* were reinforced by others. On that second day the Yankees were evicted four times from Belleu Wood but the following night they went through again in darkness and in rain. Attacks by two battalions on the 23rd at Hill 360 were broken up by trench mortar fire. In the first two days the 26th (now Bamford) had suffered 2,000 casualties.

On the 27th the 52nd Infantry Brigade (Cole) tried to go round Hill 360 through a valley to Moirey Wood on higher ground. German artillery on the rim of the bowl concentrated with great accuracy and system on the Yankees.

The Belleu Wood had still not been captured. On the northern edge the National Guardsmen and Prussians kept their heads down in fox-holes within shouting distance of each other. These outposts were well out of reach of the rolling kitchens and soldiers tossed biscuit rations from one fox-hole to another. The 29th Division, which had captured Etraye Wood (Hill 361), was relieved on 26th October by Kuhn's 79th Division. Of 5,636 casualties sustained thirty-five per cent were incurred as a result of gassing. The Belleu Wood position was not consolidated until the advance of Shelton's 51st Infantry Brigade the following day. The 79th moved in between the French 15th Colonials and the Yankee Division as they held on firmly on the southern slopes of the Borne de Cornouiller. Since the beginning of the Argonne – Meuse offensive the line had advanced five miles to the Giselhur Line. The German army might be staggering to defeat but the German units were in no mood to turn their backs on the Heights of the Meuse. Apprised of XVII Corps' objectives as an extra arm of the American First Army by talkative American prisoners, the Fifth Army braced nevertheless for a Woëvre offensive. Many divisions arriving from other sectors of the Western Front had been assembled north of Verdun. When the Supreme Command issued a number of preparatory orders for withdrawal to the Antwerp – Meuse position, Gallwitz received no new instructions. The 26th and 79th were soon to sweep over the rim of the bowl and into the Woëvre plain, which had first beckoned those eager American officers further east at St Mihiel onwards to the Rhine.

# Springboard to victory

When the western pincer was launched on 27th September four armies advanced six miles without preliminary bombardment and reached the outlying defences of the Siegfried Position. But as tanks could not precede the infantry, the British gunners opened up in earnest when Rawlinson's Fourth Army reached the St Quentin canal. In a determined attack British, Australian and American troops hurled themselves at the tunnel defences and swam the canal. By nightfall on the 29th Rawlinson had captured the first line and part of the second line of defences. Read's American II Corps, which took eighteen Medals of Honor between the canal and the Selle river, was affiliated with the Australian Corps as part of the Fourth Army. The 27th and 30th Divisions of National Guardsmen both took part in the breakthrough. All four armies were now engaged in a slow but inexorable advance. Cambrai was enveloped on the 30th and five days later the third and last position of the Hindenburg Line was in British hands. On Field Marshal Haig's left King Albert's offensive mounted on the 28th in Flanders by the Belgian, the British Second and the French Sixth Armies began well in spite of persistent rain. By 1st October the advance had progressed eight miles and succeeded in reaching the Ypres ridge. German reserves sent to face Haig weakened resistance on this sector, and the five German divisions left in Flanders could not stand up to further attack.

**The war is over. Jubilant American troops**

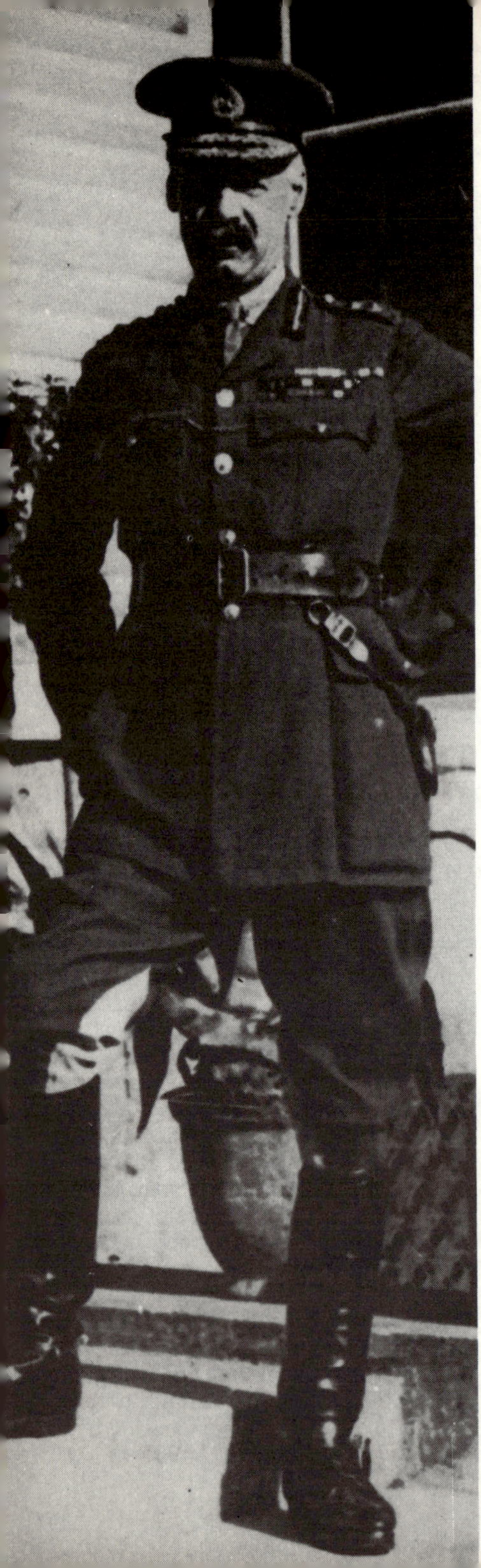

**Lieutenant-General Sir Henry Rawlinson, commander of British Fourth Army**

The rain however had turned the roads into a sea of mud and an *impasse* was reached here for a period of two weeks. Between the western pincer and the southern pincer in the Argonne, two French armies harassed the enemy to prevent the movement of their divisions to the other fronts. On the night of 28th September General Ludendorff reported to Field Marshal von Hindenburg that there was no chance of a general improvement in the German situation and that efforts to obtain an armistice should begin. German and Austrian notes proposing an armistice were accordingly forwarded to President Wilson.

Although defiant to the last Ludendorff had recognised that the crossings of the St Quentin canal and the first line of barbed-wire entrenchments in the Argonne meant that the end was in sight. When specially trained counterattack divisions failed to enthuse the rank and file infantry with the will to resist Ludendorff began to withdraw to the line of the Selle river. As will be seen, when Pershing renewed his offensive on 4th October

in the Argonne Forest and valley towards Romagne and Cunel, he was under pressure from Foch to keep pace with the *débouchement* of the British army from Siegfried; but the American First Army had still to face the horrors of Kriemhilde. St Quentin was flanked by Rawlinson's army and occupied by Debeney's French First Army. As Rawlinson and Debeney spearheaded the advance to the Selle Ludendorff fell back exhorting his reluctant troops to defend the Fatherland to the last man; and it was learned on the 13th that Wilson's 'Fourteen Points' were unacceptable to the Germans as conditions of an honourable defeat. The Foch directive stated that the objective of the southern pincer was to drive the enemy behind the Sedan – Mézières rail line before winter weather made offensive operations difficult. Pershing's third drive of 14th October was co-ordinated with the pursuit to the Selle. On Pershing's left the march of Gouraud's Fourth Army had been hampered by mine craters and shell holes, which had been created during operations of previous years. Although the French west of the Argonne ridge had advanced nine miles by 1st October, Gouraud's progress was less satisfactory than Pershing's at the beginning of the third phase of the Battle of the Argonne. And the cold comfort of late autumn in the Argonne implied that winter was not far away.

Pershing received the news of Wilson's 'Fourteen Points' over the telephone from Paris at the same time as a report that 4,000,000 Americans would be in the line in the summer of 1919. Already by mid-October the number of his troops in the Argonne and east of the Meuse had risen to just over 1,000,000 men. Asked what he thought about Wilson's plan, the general said: 'I know nothing about it. Liggett is losing no time. He is attacking tomorrow. Our business is to go on fighting until I receive orders to cease fire. We must have no other thought as soldiers.' But when Hunter Liggett took over the offensive at Kriemhilde the prospect of peace undoubtedly made the troops fight all the harder. On 17th October the Allies moved to the line of the Selle and Rawlinson's and Debeney's armies attacked the German positions from Le Cateau southwards. Horne's British First and Byng's Third Armies

**The Canadians enter Cambrai in the advance east of Arras**

went for the northern sector of the Selle position. On the French centre the line was shortened; a new army was formed and sent to Lorraine on the right of the Americans. The success of the British army in the Selle battles forced a general withdrawal. By 28th October the British First and Third occupied positions behind the Scheldt river, and King Albert experienced no further difficulties in bringing his armies into line. Laon phase of the Battle of the Argonne was highly unsatisfactory to Georges Clemenceau. Although an American division was on the Grandpré heights, the bastion of the Bourgogne Wood was still held by the German Third Army at the end of October. And between Grandpré and Brieulles the Fifth Army was still entrenched along seven miles of the Kriemhilde Line. Elsewhere the line was broken only two miles in depth, and General

A *poilu* contemplates the price of peace

fell to the French in the centre after a sweep across open country. After a period of stalemate Gouraud's Fourth Army accelerated in pace and spearheads crossed the western course of the Aisne twenty miles north of their start-line.

The slow but steady progress of the American First Army during the third

Pershing had achieved an overall advance of just ten miles. The French prime minister called yet again for the dismissal of the American Commander-in-Chief. Clemenceau had expressed disappointment in the American army on several occasions, but his displeasure did not prevent him from joining with Lloyd George and Orlando in requesting the presence of a further hundred American divisions in Europe in 1919. Of Clemenceau's

tirade Foch says: 'Having a more comprehensive knowledge of the difficulties encountered by the American army, I could not acquiesce in the radical solution contemplated by Monsieur Clemenceau.' And in a letter to Clemenceau on 23rd October: '... there is no denying the magnitude of the effort made by the American army. After attacking at St Mihiel on September 12th it attacked in the Argonne on the 26th. From September

**Hindenburg and Ludendorff realise that defeat is in sight**

26th to October 20th its losses in battle were 54,158 men – in exchange for small gains on a narrow front, it is true, but over particularly difficult terrain and in the face of serious resistance from the enemy.' And furthermore Ludendorff had been alarmed into transferring twenty-seven precious reserve divisions to

King Albert of Belgium. He commanded an army group on the extreme left flank of the Allied line

St Quentin, still under German occupation

meet the southern offensive thus facilitating the progress of the Allies in the north.

The German positions on the Scheldt had not been fortified as strongly as the Hindenburg Line or the defences of the Selle. Although as early as 20th October the German government indicated its acceptance of Wilson's terms, Ludendorff declared the armistice terms dishonourable in the eyes of the German army. The general was confident that his troops were capable of an orderly withdrawal to the line of the Meuse, and the time thus gained could be used to secure better terms. But on the instigation of the new Chancellor, Prince Max of Baden, the Kaiser informed Ludendorff of his intention of obtaining the views of other generals in the field. General Ludendorff's resignation followed immediately and he was succeeded in command of German forces on the Western Front by General Groener. Groener realistically considered the morale of the troops, lack of reserves and near collapse of the railway system and reported a rapidly deteriorating situation. Haig's task on 1st November was to force the German defences of the Scheldt. And in order to avoid the intricate dike system and difficult terrain in front of his forces, he made his principal attack south of Valenciennes using elements of the British First and Third Armies. The following day the Canadian Corps captured Valenciennes and the offensive developed strongly along a thirty-mile front. On the British right Debeney's French First Army advanced north of Guise. The fighting had been bitter, but the Scheldt positions had now definitely been turned. Meanwhile south of Ghent,

**Georges Clemenceau, the French Premier, visits the trenches. His displeasure with Pershing may partly be attributed to the latter's reluctance to allow the septuagenarian to visit Montfaucon under shell fire**

French and American units of King Albert's forces drove the Germans back from the Scheldt and Johnston's 91st Division captured Oudenarde.

The Germans withdrew all along the line, hampered by blocked roads, traffic chaos and the shortage of rail equipment. In the Fatherland German sailors mutinied at Kiel on 3rd November. Revolutionary councils of soldiers and workers, similar to those of the Bolsheviks in Russia, had been established in a number of German cities. These uprisings combined with the collapse of Austria and Turkey began to create serious unrest throughout the German nation. The British now advanced to Maubeuge and prepared to capture the enemy crossings of the Meuse from Namur to Dinant. Bavay, Avesnes and Maubeuge fell by 9th November. Soldier councils had already been formed at the front when on 8th November the Supreme Command agreed that the German army could not be relied upon to quell uprisings at home. The French armies in the centre of the advance of the British and American armies took Hirson on 9th November. On that day Prince Max of Baden announced the Kaiser's abdication, and a German republic was proclaimed. King Albert's troops joined in the pursuit, which was now extended along the entire front. Tournai and Renait were occupied and a Canadian division entered Mons a few hours before the armistice on 11th November. Meanwhile the American First Army was breaking out from the Argonne. General Pershing declared that the fighting should continue until the German forces were obliged to lay

**Nascent revolution in Berlin and other German cities seriously undermined the will to resist at the front**

down their arms in the field; but Marshal Foch's view was that additional bloodshed was unnecessary if the terms of the Armistice were sufficiently rigorous to deprive Germany of the ability to continue the war.

When Ludendorff talked of holding the Antwerp – Meuse line, Prince Max agreed that the Americans must be prevented from advancing north of Verdun. In the Argonne on 1st November Liggett's First Army was still arranged from I Corps on the left through V Corps to III Corps on the right.

At 0530 hours on the foggy November morning army artillery rolled a barrage across a zone 1,200 yards in depth. Although Dickman's corps on the left did not start well, the enemy was driven from Loges Wood and Champigneulle on the second day and the American troops went hurrying through the Bourgogne Wood. Six miles on Buzancy also fell on 2nd November. On the next day Dickman drove five miles through the German lines, and joined forces with the French Fourth Army beyond the Bourgogne Wood. This advance brought the rail line running southeast from Sedan within range of American artillery and guns quickly pounded the rail centres of Montmédy and Longuyon. Summerall's V Corps in possession of the woods and Heights of Barricourt faced the ultimate crest of the Argonne barrier. The 89th was thrown straight at the crest and once on top the way was clear to the Meuse. Hines' III Corps swung from the high ground and went straight for the river. The 90th on the night of 2nd November had Villers – Devant – Dun and Hill 212. The regular 5th Division took Cléry-Petit, a mile down river from Brieulles, on the forenoon of the same day. The line on 3rd November showed a bulge projecting southwards almost to Beaumont where a brigade

**'Calamity Jane', the last gun fired on the American front on 11th November 1918**

of the 2nd Division captured Germans in their billets after taking La Tuilerie farm about midnight.

The 79th stormed the Borne de Cornouiller, and the Yankee Division, co-operating with the French, went forward in a line of brigades through the woods north of Verdun. The 42nd Division, which now became the extreme left of the American line, headed directly towards Sedan with its left tangent to the boundary with the French just east of the La Bar river. When Liggett ordered the whole of III Corps across the Meuse, the First Army made a broad sweep along a thirty-mile front. Further east Bullard's American Second Army flanked by French forces prepared to advance north of St Mihiel across the Woëvre plain to Briey and its ironfields. On the left and centre of the First Army the advance was impeded by shelling and problems of supply created by traffic disorder. A proper quota of tanks at this time would have cut off 100,000 German troops retreating across the Meuse southeast of Sedan. But General Pershing's wish that the First Army should have the honour of taking Sedan all but led to monumental tragedy. Although Sedan lay within the French zone of command, the American request was prompted by the fact that on 5th November Liggett was well ahead of Gouraud's Fourth Army on the left. General Maistre, who was co-ordinating activity along the boundary, surprisingly agreed to the American Commander-in-Chief's request. After the Chief of Operations for First Army Colonel George C Marshall, Jr, addressed an ambiguously worded operations order to *both* I and V Corps, the race for Sedan began.

The French army's most ardent ambition as the war drew to a close was to capture Sedan and avenge its humiliating defeat there at the hands of the Prussians in 1870. This event was not unconnected with the origins of the Great War, and Pershing's request may be compared in audacity to Lafayette or de Rochambeau perhaps taking the salute at Yorktown. On the 6th General Summerall went personally to McGlachlin's 1st Division command post and gave a verbal order for the men to march immediately to the city. Formed up in five columns the 1st now began a forced march through the night using various roads across the lines of advance of Dickman's I Corps. When the left corps commander heard what was happening he alerted the 42nd and 77th Divisions lest their guns fire on units of the 1st Division traversing their paths. The march completely demoralized the communication and supply of I Corps and confused the advance of their two spearhead divisions. Worse was to come. On representation from General Gouraud, Marshal Foch, the Maistre agreement notwithstanding, declared the Fourth Army boundary inviolate. Early on the 7th General Dickman was informed that unless an American regiment forming the left column of the 1st under Lieutenant-Colonel

Roosevelt was withdrawn within the hour from the Fourth Army zone, French guns would open fire on American troops. Later that day troops of both the exhausted 1st and 42nd Divisions stood back on the Sedan heights at Pont-Maugis and watched the French streaming into the city.

The Lille – Metz supply line had been crossed at Avesnes west of Maubeuge, Hirson and Sedan, and the railway was under fire further south at Montmédy. Mézières, the objective of the southern offensive, lies ten miles west of Sedan and was taken by the Fourth Army. The Foch Plan was thus realised although the pincer grip did not close tight but, defeated by political as well as by military manoeuvre, the question of the Germans defending the Fatherland did not arise. General Pershing arrived in Chaumont on the night of the 10th and received word from Marshal Foch at 0600 hours the following morning that hostilities would cease five hours later. On 11th November the American First and Second Armies were linked along a one hundred mile front from Pont-Maugis near Sedan south-eastwards through Fresnes-en-Woëvre to Port-sur-Seilles south of Metz. Since 26th September the American army had advanced thirty-two miles from their start-line in the Argonne. During that time twenty-two American and six French divisions, with an approximate combat strength of 500,000 men, were engaged on a front extending from the Argonne forest to the Meuse heights south-east of Verdun. They decisively defeated forty-three German and Austrian Divisions with a fighting strength of 470,000 men. The Germans suffered an estimated loss of over 100,000 casualties in battle, and the First Army about 117,000. The total strength of the First Army reached 1,031,000 men. The Americans captured 26,000 prisoners, 874 cannon, 3,000 machine-guns and large quantities of *matériel*.

**General Pershing leads a victory parade on 14th July 1919 in Paris**

# Bibliography

*The Genesis of the American First Army*, prepared in the Historical Section Army War College, United States Government Printing Office, Washington
*Sergeant York: His Own Life Story and War Diary* by Tom Skeyhill (Doubleday, Doran & Co, New York)
*Histories of Two Hundred and Fifty-one Divisions of the German Army which participated in the War, 1914-18.* Compiled from the records of the Intelligence Section of the General Staff, American Expeditionary Forces 1919, Washington
*America in France: the Story of the Making of an Army* by Frederick Palmer (John Murray, London)
*America's Munitions, 1917-1918*, report by B Crowell, Washington
*The American Army in France 1917-1919* by James G Harbord (Little, Brown & Co, Boston)
*Order of Battle of the United States Land Forces in the World War (American Expeditionary Forces)*, Washington
*My Experiences in the World War* by John J Pershing (F Stokes Co, New York)
*As They Saw Us. Foch, Ludendorff and other Leaders write our War History* by G S Vierek the Elder (ed) with the assistance of A Paul Maerker-Branden (Doubleday, Doran & Co, New York)

\* \* \* \*

*And don't miss Ballantine's best-selling standard-size War Books*—most with 16 pages of photos—$1.25 each:

COMPANY COMMANDER
Charles B. MacDonald

JAPANESE DESTROYER CAPTAIN
Capt. Tameichi Hara with
Fred Saito and Roger Pineau

SECRET WEAPONS OF WW II
Gerald Pawle

THE GREATEST ACES
Edward B. Sims

THE BATTLE OF THE BULGE
Robert Merriam

FORTY-EIGHT HOURS TO HAMMELBURG
Charles Whiting

WITH ROMMEL IN THE DESERT
H. W. Schmidt

QUEEN OF THE FLAT-TOPS
Stanley Johnston

THE SEA WOLVES
Wolfgang Frank

THE LIFE AND DEATH OF THE LUFTWAFFE
Werner Baumbach

THE RAGGED, RUGGED WARRIORS
Martin Caidin

ROMMEL
Ronald Lewin

GREY WOLF, GREY SEA
E. B. Gasaway

SAMURAI
Saburo Sakai with Martin Caidin
and Fred Saito

THE DIVINE WIND
Rikihei Inoguchi, Tadashi Nakajima
and Roger Pineau

Send for our catalog: to Dept. CS, Ballantine Books, Inc.,
36 West 20th Street, New York, N.Y. 10003

All volumes of Ballantine's Illustrated History of the Violent Century are only $1.00, except NAZI REGALIA in full-color at $2.95.